BRAIDING
AND KNOTTING

TECHNIQUES AND PROJECTS

B Y

Constantine A. Belash

Illustrations by
CHARLES E. WHITE, JR.

DOVER PUBLICATIONS, INC.

NEW YORK

Published in Canada by General Publishing Company, Ltd., 30 Lesmill Road, Don Mills, Toronto, Ontario.

This Dover edition, first published in 1974, is an unabridged republication of the work originally published by the Beacon Press, Inc., in Boston, in 1936. The text has not been abridged, but a brief Foreword and Preface which appeared in the 1936 edition have been omitted in this Dover edition.

International Standard Book Number: 0-486-23059-7
Library of Congress Catalog Card Number: 74-75266

Manufactured in the United States of America
Dover Publications, Inc.
180 Varick Street
New York, N.Y. 10014

TABLE OF CONTENTS

PART I

BRAIDING

iii

TABLE OF CONTENTS

PART I   BRAIDING

CHAPTER I

General Directions for Braiding

Instinctive Use of Braiding

THE process of braiding strands together, both for decorative effect and in order to obtain added strength, seems to have been one of man's earliest accomplishments. It may even have been that, through braiding, he was led to discover the more intricate art of weaving—an art developed by all the earliest civilizations, thousands of years ago. Because of the perishableness of braiding materials and the fact that no tools are used in the process, there can be no historic evidence to substantiate this theory.

The process of braiding applied to the hair can be more definitely traced. It is known that both men and women of long-haired races used to braid their hair in remote prehistoric times, either in one or two wide plaits or, as in the case of the early Egyptians, in a great number of small, tight braids. In Greece, the earliest center of European culture, men were wearing their hair in elaborate arrangements in the sixth century B. C., but, under the influence of the unrivalled Greek sculptors of the fourth century, the custom was introduced for men to have their hair cut short. The Romans quickly adopted the Greek style and short hair for men was continued in Europe under the Roman Republic and Empire and through the Middle Ages. In the seventeenth century A. D., long hair again became fashionable for men and, by the year 1680, had led to the wearing of large braided and curled wigs by both men and women of the wealthy classes. England followed the fashion of the Continent and the British soldiers in the American Revolution almost all had long braids, which they larded and powdered or wore in eel skins. In the early part of the nineteenth century, the fashion was dropped.

In the periods when men have worn their hair long, they seem to have taken great pride in their braids and curls, the only exception being for the queues of the Chinese. Previous to the year 1644, Chinese men, and also their neighbors in Japan and Korea, were wearing their hair long and done in a knot at the back of the head. In that year, with the establishment of the Manchu dynasty as a result of a rebellion which overthrew the ruling Ming dynasty, there was introduced into China the odd style of the Manchus of shaving the front part of the head and allowing the rest of the hair to grow long, and braiding the long hair in a queue, lengthened, if need be, with black silk or false hair, to reach below the knee. The custom was not generally adopted by native Chinese until, in 1864, after a rebellion against Manchu authority had been suppressed, an edict was issued requiring all Chinese men to wear their hair in queues as a symbol of submission. It is recorded that more than a million men suffered themselves to be put to death rather than submit to the humiliation. The edict was kept in force until the revolution in 1912 and the establishment of the Chinese Republic, when it was immediately revoked and men were allowed to wear their hair short in the European and American fashion, which had already been adopted by the Japanese and Koreans. The Chinese queues furnish the only known example of braids' being used as marks of disgrace.

This summary has been given in order to show how

the braiding of hair, almost universally by women until within a few years and recurrently by men, has been an instinctive impulse of the human race. But even by primitive people braiding was also early applied to other materials, such as long native grasses and weeds, or strips of palm or banana leaves in Africa and the East Indies, which were braided together for strength or even made into baskets at a very early date. That the ornamental use of braiding was especially emphasized is shown in our language by the fact that the word "braid" is applied to any narrow decorative strip, whether or not made by the process of braiding. The various methods of braiding used today to give extra strength, for decorative purposes, and for making into articles, some of which have been known and practiced for many centuries, will be described in the following pages.

Materials for Braiding

Any material which can be made into strips and is flexible can be hand-braided. To the grasses and weeds already mentioned may be added an almost limitless list of suitable materials, such as string, cord, paper, cloth, leather, and even thin strips of metal. Different materials may even be braided together, or several strips of a fine material, like raffia, may be used together for each strand, but the strands should all be of the same thickness to make the braiding even. Various patterns and attractive effects can be obtained by using strands of different colors.

Securing Braiding Strands

The ends of strands should be fastened securely before the braid is started, so that they will not slip out of place.

It is usually most convenient to tie the ends together with a piece of string, but it is often advisable to keep them flat. Strands of cloth or similar materials may be pinned separately onto a heavy cushion. The ends of strings or cords may be placed in position on a moistened strip of gummed paper, the gummed paper then folded over them and the covered ends inserted in a strong paper clip. This is the method which has been used for the illustrations of braids in the following chapters.

After the ends have been made secure, the work should be attached to a vise or other steady object so that the strands can be held taut during the braiding. Closing the end of a braid into a table drawer is also a convenient method of holding the work.

Preventing Tangling of Strands

If long strands of braiding material are being used, each strand should be rolled loosely and secured with a rubber band to prevent the ends from becoming tangled. If the strands are not rolled and a tangle results, pulling one strand out of the tangle will loosen the other strands also.

Joining Strands

The methods of joining strands, when added length is needed, vary with the materials used. Grasses and fibers, like raffia, may be joined by merely laying a new length on top of the short end of the old strand, when it is in the center of the braid, but never when it is on an outer edge. The braiding is then continued, with the new strand on top of the old one, for several inches until it is securely in place, when the short ends may be cut off. Strips of cloth should be sewed together, usually by a diagonal seam, on the wrong side. Strings and cords may be spliced for joining. The ends of both the old and new strands should be unravelled for about an inch. Then the little threads of the new end should be twisted with the threads of the old end. A little paste or rubber cement may be used to hold the threads in position.

In joining leather strands, the end of the used strand should be shaved off, or "skived," diagonally on the under side and the new strand shaved off at the same angle but in the opposite direction on the upper side. The end of the old strand should then be placed on top of the new end, with a little of some kind of adhesive to hold it in place, and the join allowed to dry under pressure before the braiding is continued.

Tension for Braiding

Braiding may be done loosely or tightly, as preferred for the use intended, but usually rather firm braiding is preferable. In any case, the tension should be maintained consistently throughout the braid and the strands should be kept at a uniform slant. Care should also be taken not to twist the strands, which is especially likely to happen on the edges. This is particularly to be avoided when the under side of the strand is seamed or unfinished.

Though braiding processes are all comparatively simple, it is necessary that the work should be done carefully, as any errors are very noticeable. Accuracy, therefore, and uniformity of tension are the most important factors for attractive braiding.

CHAPTER II

FLAT BRAIDING

FLAT braiding consists primarily of bringing the outer left and the outer right strands over or under one or more adjoining strands. The braiding of first the outer left strand and then the outer right, or vice versa, constitutes one row of braiding. In the next row, the second strand of the preceding row will have become the outer left and the next to the last strand of the preceding row will have become the outer right. These strands, therefore, are the working strands for this row. The process is continued until the braid is of the desired length.

Strips of any flexible material may be used for flat braiding. Some of the suitable materials are suggested on page 3. A great variety of effects may be obtained by braiding with strands of two or more different colors, the greater the number of strands used for the braid, the greater the diversity of the possible effects.

The braids used for the illustrations of the flat-braiding processes were made of smooth-finished twine. The strands were all of the same color; one or more strands have been shaded in the plates in order to bring out the process more clearly.

Simplest Method of Flat Braiding

The illustrations in Plate I show the simplest form of braiding, first with the outer left strand and then with the outer right strand. (The steps may be reversed, if preferred, beginning with the outer right, followed by the outer left.)

A. *Three strands*. Bring the outer left strand, No. 1 of Figure A, to the right over No. 2, so that strand No. 1 is next to No. 3. Then bring the outer right strand No. 3, to the left over No. 1, so that No. 3 is next to

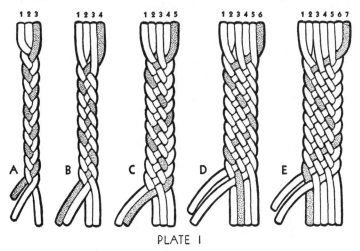

PLATE I

No. 2. These two steps complete the first row of braiding. To continue, repeat these two steps: bring the outer left strand, over the strand at its right; then bring the outer right strand, over the strand at its left.

B. *Four strands*. Bring the outer left strand, No. 1 in Figure B, over No. 2, so that No. 1 is next to No. 3. Then bring the outer right strand, No. 4, under No. 3 and over No. 1, so that No. 4 is next to No. 2. To continue, repeat these two steps: bring the outer left strand over the strand at its right; then bring the outer right strand under the strand at its left and over the next strand.

C. *Five strands.* Bring the outer left strand, No. 1 in Figure C, over No. 2, so that No. 1 is next to No. 3. Then bring the outer right strand, No. 5, over No. 4, under No. 3, and over No. 1, so that No. 5 is next to No. 2. To continue, repeat these two steps: bring the outer left strand over the strand at its right; then bring the outer right strand over the strand at its left, under the next strand, and over the next one.

In adapting this method of braiding to a greater number of strands, the two steps will be done in the same way as has been described. The first step—bringing the outer left strand over the strand at its right—is always the same. For the second step, if you are braiding with an odd number of strands (3, 5, 7, 9, 11, etc.) the outer right strand is brought over the strand at its left; whereas, if you are braiding with an even number of strands (4, 6, 8, 10, 12, etc.) the outer right strand is brought under the strand at its left.

Variation of First Method

The process of braiding shown in the illustrations of Plate II is somewhat different from the first method, illustrated in Plate I, though the braids are similar in appearance. The steps in three-strand and four-strand braiding are the same as in the first method, and may be considered as either under the first method or under this method of braiding.

A. *Five Strands.* Bring the outer left strand, No. 1 in Figure A, over No. 2 and under No. 3, so that No. 1 is next to No. 4. Then bring the outer right strand, No. 5, over No. 4 and under No. 1, so that No. 5 is next to No. 3. To continue: bring the outer left strand over the strand at its right and under the next strand; then bring the outer right strand over the strand at its left and under the next strand.

B ¹. *Six strands.* (*First method of starting.*) Bring the outer left strand, No. 1 in Figure B ¹, over No. 2 and under No. 3, so that No. 1 is next to No. 4. Then bring

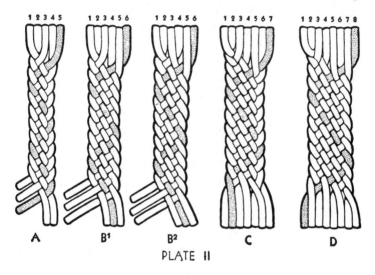

PLATE II

the outer right strand, No. 6, under No. 5, over No. 4, and under No. 1, so that No. 6 is next to No. 3. To continue: bring the outer left strand over the strand at its right and under the next strand; then bring the outer right strand under the strand at its left, over the next strand, and under the next one.

B ². *Six strands.* (*Second method of starting.*) Bring the outer left strand No. 1 in Figure B ², over No. 2, so that No. 1 is next to No. 3. Then bring the third strand, No. 3, over No. 4 and bring No. 4 to the left over No. 1, so that No. 4 is next to No. 2. Then bring No. 5 over No. 6, and bring No. 6 to the left over No. 3 and under No. 1. You will then have three strands, Nos. 2, 4, and 6, at the left, and the other three strands, Nos. 1, 3, and 5, at the right. To continue: bring the outer left strand over the strand at its right and under the next strand so that it is next to the lowest right strand. Then bring the outer right strand under the strand at its left, over the next strand, and under the next, so that it is next to the lowest left strand.

This method of braiding may be used with any number of strands. If you are braiding an odd number of strands (5, 7, 9, 11, etc.), there is only one method of starting the braiding; if you are braiding with an even number of strands (6, 8, 10, 12, etc.), there are two methods of starting, as described for six strands, the second method usually being preferable.

This method of braiding will always come to a point in the center. If you wish a straight edge in finishing, braid the left and right sides down without carrying the strands across the center strands, as shown in Figures C and D.

Braiding over One or More Double Strands

The braiding strand may be carried over or under two neighboring strands, which are kept together as a double strand, as shown in Plate III. This is especially useful in adding strength to the braid. In making such a braid, one pair of strands may be used as a double strand, while all the other strands are kept single, or two or more double strands may be used. Some of the possible combinations are described and illustrated.

A. *Four strands.* Bring the outer left strand, No. 1 in Figure A, over both No. 2 and No. 3, so that No. 1 is

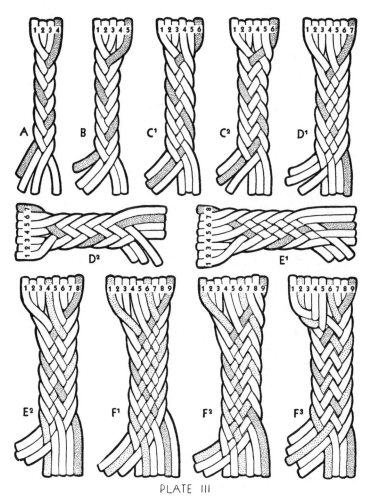

PLATE III

next to No. 4. Then bring the outer right strand, No. 4, over No. 1, so that No. 4 is next to No. 3. To continue: bring the outer left strand over both the strand at its right and the next strand also; then bring the outer right strand over one strand at its left. This will look like regular three-strand braiding except that the left edge will be thicker than the right.

B. *Five strands*. Bring the outer left strand, No. 1 in Figure B, over both No. 2 and No. 3, so that No. 1 is next to No. 4. Then bring the outer right strand, No. 5, over both No. 4 and No. 1, so that No. 5 is next to No. 3. To continue: bring the outer left strand over both the strand at its right and the next strand also; then bring the outer right strand over both the strand at its left and the next strand also.

C¹. *Six strands*. Bring the outer left strand, No. 1 in Figure C¹, over both No. 2 and No. 3, so that No. 1 is next to No. 4. Then bring the outer right strand, No. 6, under both No. 5 and No. 4 and over No. 1, so that No. 6 is next to No. 3. To continue: bring the outer left strand over both the strand at its right and the next strand also; then bring the outer left strand under both the strand at its left and the next strand also and then over the next strand.

C². *Six strands*. Bring the outer left strand, No. 1 in Figure C², over both No. 2 and No. 3, as in the preceding method. Then bring the outer right strand, No. 6, under No. 5 and then over both No. 4 and No. 1, so that No. 6 is next to No. 3. To continue: bring the outer left strand over both the strand at its right and the next strand also; then bring the outer right strand under the strand at its left, and then over the next two strands.

D¹. *Seven strands*. Bring the outer left strand, No. 1 in Figure D¹, over both No. 2 and No. 3, so that No. 1 is next to No. 4. Then bring the outer right strand, No. 7, over both No. 6 and No. 5, under No. 4, and over No. 1, so that No. 7 is next to No. 3. To continue: bring the outer left strand over both the strand at its right and the next strand also; then bring the outer right strand over both the strand at its left and the next strand also, then under the next strand, and over the next one.

D². *Seven strands.* Bring the outer left strand, No. 1 in Figure D², over both No. 2 and No. 3, so that No. 1 is next to No. 4. Then bring the outer right strand, No. 7, under both No. 6 and No. 5 and over both No. 4 and No. 1, so that No. 7 is next to No. 3. To continue: bring the outer left strand over both the strand at its right and the next strand also; then bring the outer right strand under both the strand at its left and the next strand also, then over the next two strands.

E¹. *Eight strands.* Bring the outer left strand, No. 1 in Figure E¹, over both the strand at its right and the next strand also; then bring the outer right strand under both the strand at its left and the next strand also; then over the next strand, under the next, and over the next.

E². *Eight strands.* Bring the outer left strand, No. 1 in Figure E², over both the strand at its right and the next strand also; then bring the outer right strand over both the strand at its left and the next strand also, then under the next two strands, and over the next strand.

F¹. *Nine strands.* Bring the outer left strand, No. 1 in Figure F¹, over both the strand at its right and the next strand also; then bring the outer right strand over the strand at its left and the next strand also, then under the next strand, over the next, under the next, and over the next.

F². *Nine strands.* Bring the outer left strand, No. 1 in Figure F², over both the strand at its right and the next strand also; then bring the outer right strand under the strand at its left and the next strand also, then over the next two strands, under the next strand, and over the next one.

F³. *Nine strands.* Bring the outer left strand, No. 1 in Figure F³, over both the strand at its right and the next strand also, then under the next two strands; then bring the outer right strand over both the strand at its left and the next strand also, then under the next two strands.

The process is applicable to any number of strands. The braiding strands are single, but one or more pairs of neighboring strands may be crossed over or under as a double strand.

Braiding over One or More Triple Strands

In the preceding directions, the braiding strands were brought across two neighboring strands treated together as a double strand. Three neighboring strands may be similarly used as a triple strand. Some of the possible combinations are shown in Plate IV.

A. *Five strands.* Bring the outer left strand, No. 1 in Figure A, over Nos. 2, 3, and 4, so that No. 1 is next to No. 5. Then bring the outer right strand, No. 5, over No. 1 so that No. 5 is next to No. 4. To continue: bring the outer left strand over three strands at its right; then bring the outer right strand over one strand at its left.

B¹. *Six strands.* Bring the outer left strand, No. 1 in Figure B¹, over Nos. 2, 3, and 4, so that No. 1 is next to No. 5. Then bring the outer right strand, No. 6, under No. 5 and over No. 1, so that No. 6 is next to No. 4. To continue: bring the outer left strand over three strands at its right; then bring the outer right strand under the strand at its left and over the next strand.

B². *Six strands.* Bring the outer left strand, No. 1 in

Figure B², over Nos. 2, 3, and 4, as in the preceding directions. Then bring the outer right strand, No. 6, over both No. 5 and No. 1, so that No. 6 is next to No. 4.

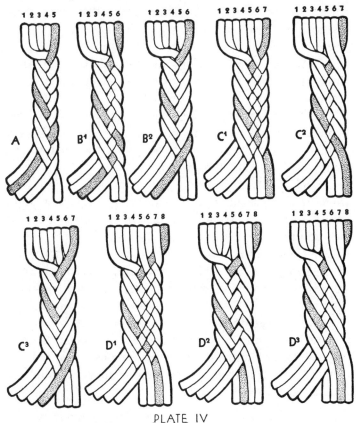

PLATE IV

To continue: bring the outer left strand over three strands at its right; then bring the outer right strand over two strands at its left.

C¹. *Seven strands*. Bring the outer left strand over three strands at its right; then bring the outer right strand over the strand at its left, under the next strand, and over the next one.

C². *Seven strands.* Bring the outer left strand over three strands at its right; then bring the outer right strand under two strands at its left and over the next one.

C³. *Seven strands.* Bring the outer left strand over three strands at its right; then bring the outer right strand over three strands at its left.

D¹. *Eight strands.* Bring the outer left strand over three strands at its right; then bring the outer right strand under the strand at its left, over the next strand, under the next, and over the next.

D². *Eight strands.* Bring the outer left strand over three strands at its right; then bring the outer right strand under two strands at its left and over the next two strands.

D³. *Eight strands.* Bring the outer left strand over three strands at its right; then bring the outer right strand under three strands at its left and over the next one.

Braiding over double or triple strands may be applied to any larger number of strands by processes similar to those already described. When the strands are of narrow material, even four or more strands may be similarly grouped together.

Braiding with Double Working Strands

The preceding methods have all described the use of single braiding strands brought over one strand at a time in methods I and II, over single and double strands in III, and over single, double, and triple strands in IV.

Plate V shows the use of double, instead of single, braiding strands.

A. *Four strands*. Bring the outer left strand, No. 1 in Figure A, and No. 2 together over No. 3. Then bring the outer right strand, No. 4, over both No. 2 and No. 1.

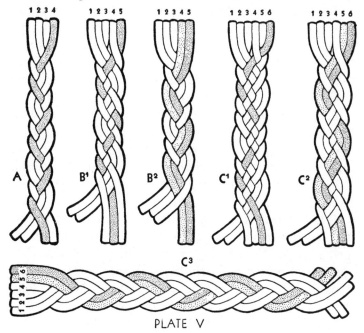

PLATE V

Continue the braiding as in simple three-strand braiding (Plate I, Figure A), keeping Nos. 1 and 2 together as a double strand. Where strands of different colors are used, different effects may be obtained by having No. 1 a single strand and Nos. 2 and 3 together as a double strand and No. 4 single; or No. 1 single, No. 2 single, and Nos. 3 and 4 together as a double strand.

B¹. *Five strands*. Bring strands Nos. 1 and 2 in Figure B¹ together over No. 3. Then bring the outer right strand, No. 5, under No. 4 and over both No. 1 and No. 2. Continue as in four-strand braiding (Plate I, Figure B), using No. 1 and No. 2 together as a double strand.

B². *Five strands*. Bring strands Nos. 1 and 2 in Figure B² together over No. 3. Then bring Nos. 4 and 5 together over both No. 2 and No. 1. Continue as in three-strand braiding (Plate I, Figure A), using No. 1 and No. 2 together as a double strand, No. 3 single, and No. 4 and No. 5 together as a double strand.

C¹. *Six strands*. Bring strands Nos. 1 and 2 in Figure C¹ together over No. 3. Then bring the outer right strand, No. 6, over No. 5, under No. 4, and over both No. 2 and No. 1. Continue as in five-strand braiding (Plate I, Figure C), using Nos. 1 and 2 together as a double strand.

C². *Six strands*. Bring strands Nos. 1 and 2 in Figure C² together over No. 3. Then bring Nos. 5 and 6 together under No. 4 and over both No. 2 and No. 1. Continue as in four-strand braiding (Plate I, Figure B), using Nos. 1 and 2 together as a double strand, No. 3 single, No. 4 single, and Nos. 5 and 6 double.

C³. *Six strands*. Bring strands Nos. 1 and 2 in Figure C³ together over both No. 3 and No. 4. Then bring No. 5 and No. 6 together over both No. 2 and No. 1. Continue as in three-strand braiding (Plate I, Figure A), using three sets of double strands.

In any of these braids, any two neighboring strands may be used as a double strand, as was suggested for four strands. The same method may be used with any higher number of strands.

Braiding with Triple Working Strands

Three neighboring strands may be used together as a triple strand in the same manner as double strands were used in the preceding method. Some of the possible combinations are shown in Plate VI.

A. *Five strands.* Bring strands Nos. 1, 2, and 3 in Figure A together over No. 4. Then bring strand No. 5 over Nos. 3, 2 and 1. Continue as in three-strand braiding (Plate I, Figure A), using Nos. 1, 2 and 3 together as a triple strand and the other two strands single.

B ^{1}. *Six strands.* Bring strands Nos. 1, 2, and 3 in Figure B ^{1} together over No. 4. Then bring strand No. 6 under No. 5 and over Nos. 3, 2, and 1. Continue as in four-strand braiding (Plate I, Figure B), using Nos. 1, 2, and 3 together as a triple strand and the other three strands single.

B ^{2}. *Six strands.* Bring strands Nos. 1, 2, and 3 in Figure B ^{2} over No. 4. Then bring strands Nos. 6 and 5 together over Nos. 3, 2, and 1. Continue as in three-strand braiding (Plate I, Figure A), using Nos. 1, 2, and 3 as a triple strand, No. 4 single, and Nos. 5 and 6 as a double strand.

C ^{1}. *Seven strands.* Bring strands Nos. 1, 2, and 3 in Figure C ^{1} together over No. 4. Then bring strand No. 7 over No. 6, under No. 5, and over Nos. 3, 2, and 1. Continue as in five-strand braiding (Plate I, Figure C), using strands Nos. 1, 2, and 3 as a triple strand and the other four strands single.

C ^{2}. *Seven strands.* Bring strands Nos. 1, 2, and 3 in Figure C ^{2} together over No. 4. Then bring strands Nos. 7 and 6 together under No. 5, and over Nos. 3, 2, and 1.

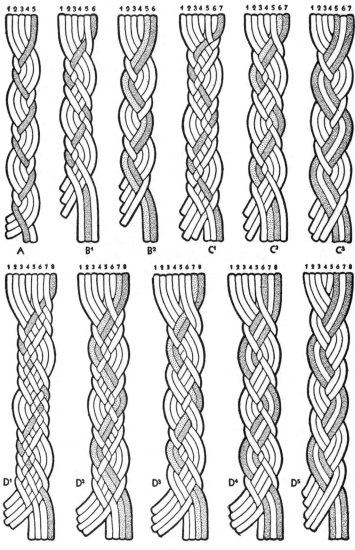

PLATE VI

Continue as in four-strand braiding (Plate I, Figure B), using Nos. 1, 2, and 3 together as a triple strand, No. 4, single, No. 5 single, and Nos. 6 and 7 together as a double strand.

C³. *Seven strands.* Bring strands Nos. 1, 2, and 3 in Figure C³ together over No. 4. Then bring Nos. 5, 6, and 7 together over Nos. 3, 2, and 1. Continue as in three-strand braiding (Plate I, Figure A), using strands Nos. 1, 2, and 3 together as a triple strand, No. 4 single, and Nos. 5, 6, and 7 together as a triple strand.

D¹. *Eight strands.* Bring strands Nos. 1, 2, and 3 in Figure D¹ over No. 4. Then bring strand No. 8 under No. 7, over No. 6, under No. 5, and over Nos. 3, 2, and 1. Continue as in six-strand braiding (Plate I, Figure D), using Nos. 1, 2, and 3 together as a triple strand and the other five strands single.

D². *Eight strands.* Bring strands Nos. 1, 2, and 3 in Figure D² together over No. 4. Then bring Nos. 7 and 8 together over No. 6, under No. 5, and over Nos. 3, 2, and 1. Continue as in five-strand braiding (Plate I, Figure C), using strands Nos. 1, 2, and 3 together as a triple strand, No. 4 single, No. 5 single, No. 6 single, and Nos. 7 and 8 together as a double strand.

D³ *Eight strands.* Bring strands Nos. 1, 2, and 3 in Figure D³ together over No. 4. Then bring Nos. 7 and 8 together under both No. 6 and No. 5, and over Nos. 3, 2, and 1. Continue as in four-strand braiding (Plate I, Figure B), using strands Nos. 1, 2, and 3 together as a triple strand, No. 4 single, Nos. 5 and 6 together as a double strand, and Nos. 7 and 8 together as a double strand.

D⁴. *Eight strands.* Bring strands Nos. 1, 2, and 3 in Figure D⁴ together over No. 4. Then bring strands Nos.

6, 7, and 8 together under No. 5 and over Nos. 3, 2, and 1. Continue as in four-strand braiding (Plate I, Figure B), using Nos. 1, 2, and 3 together as a triple strand, No. 4 single, No. 5 single, and Nos. 6, 7, and 8 together as a triple strand.

D⁵. *Eight strands.* Bring strands Nos. 1, 2, and 3 in Figure D⁵ together over both Nos. 4 and 5. Then bring Nos. 6, 7, and 8 together over Nos. 3, 2, and 1. Continue as in three-strand braiding (Plate I, Figure A), using strands Nos. 1, 2, and 3 together as a triple strand, Nos. 4 and 5 together as a double strand, and Nos. 6, 7, and 8 together as a triple strand.

These same processes may be applied to braids of higher numbers of strands, the variety of possible combinations increasing with the number of strands.

If you are using strands of material which is narrow and very flexible, even four or more neighboring strands may be grouped and used together.

Dividing and Rejoining a Braid

It is sometimes desirable to divide braids of six or more strands into smaller braids and then rejoin them again into one braid, as shown in Plate VII. This may be for decorative effect or to make an opening in the braid through which a button or another braid may be passed.

A. *Six strands.* The braiding may be started with any method of six-strand braiding. When you wish to divide the braid, have three strands on the left of the center and the three other strands on the right. Secure the right group of three strands with a paper clip or tie with a piece of string, while you braid the three left strands to the desired length. Then secure the end of the little

braid, while you braid the three right strands. In braiding
the right group, the braiding strands must be passed
under, instead of over, the middle strand. When both
braids are of the desired length, they are rejoined by
passing the outer right strand of the left braid over the
outer left strand of the right braid. (Figure A.) Then
bring the middle strand of the left braid under the outer

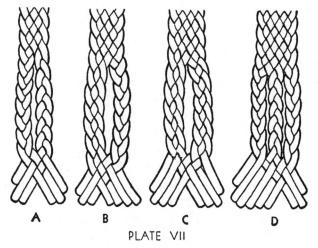

PLATE VII

left strand of the right braid and over the middle strand.
Continue with the same method of six-strand braiding
as was used at the beginning.

B. *Seven strands.* A seven-strand braid may be divided
into one braid of four strands and one of three strands.
Braid with any method of seven-strand braiding until
you wish to divide the braid. Then use the four strands
at the left of the center for regular four-strand braiding and the three strands at the right for regular three-
strand braiding (or vice versa). To rejoin the small braids,
first bring the outer right strand of the left braid under

the outer left strand of the right braid and then weave the strands over or under one another until they are in position to continue. (Figure B.)

C. *Eight strands.* A braid of eight strands may be divided into two four-strand braids. Braid with any eight-strand method until you wish to divide the braid. Use the four strands at the left of the center for the left small braid, and the four strands at the right for the right small braid. To rejoin the braids, weave the two strands at the right of the left small braid through the two strands at the left of the right small braid and weave the other strands over or under one another until they are in position to continue the eight-strand braiding. (Figure C.)

A braid of eight strands may also be divided into a braid of five strands and a braid of three strands.

D. *Nine strands.* Braids of nine strands may be divided into three small three-strand braids. When the strands are divided in this way, the three strands at the left are to be braided by regular three-strand braiding; in braiding the three middle strands, the braiding strands must be passed under, instead of over the center strand; the right three-strand braid is to be done regularly. To rejoin the three small braids, first bring the outer right strand of the first braid over the outer left strand of the second. Then bring the outer left strand of the third braid over the outer right strand of the second and under the outer right strand of the first braid. (Figure D.) Then bring the outer right strand of the third braid over the middle strand of the same braid, under the strand which was the outer right of the second braid and over the strand which was the outer right of the first braid. The process of weaving these strands into each other will have to be varied a little from the directions given, if the strands at the ends of your braids are not in the positions shown. The principle, however, is the same.

Braids of nine strands may also be divided into two smaller braids, one of six strands and the other of three, or one of five strands and the other of four.

Braids of more than nine strands may be similarly divided into two or more smaller braids of three or more strands. Any of the methods applicable may be used both in the principal braid and in the small braids into which it is divided.

CHAPTER III

WEAVING OVER STATIONARY STRANDS

IN the methods of braiding described in the preceding chapter, the process consisted of bringing the outer left and outer right strands as working strands over or under neighboring strands to the middle of the braid, thus leaving new outer left and outer right strands to be used as the working strands for the next row of work. As the braiding continued, therefore, all the strands in their turn became working strands.

Differing from this process is the method in which one or more of the strands are always kept stationary in a vertical position, while the other strand or strands are woven across them. The weaving strands must necessarily be much longer than the vertical strands. In this method, if the weaving strands are folded over or under the outer left and right vertical strands, they will be wrong side up when being returned from the opposite side to their original positions. If the braiding material has an unfinished or seamed wrong side, the weaving strands can be kept right side up by making flat loops at the turns on the sides. To tighten the work, stop after every inch or so and, holding the vertical strands tight, push up the cross strands close together.

One Strand Woven across Stationary Strands

A single strand may be woven across one or more vertical strands, as shown in Plate VIII. Either the outer

left or the outer right strand may be used as the working
strand. The illustrations show the outer left strand so
used. It may be folded over or under the outer right and
left vertical strands, as in Figures A and E, or it may be
kept flat, as in Figures B, C, and D.

A. *Three strands.* Bring the outer left strand, No. 1 in
Figure A, over No. 2 and under No. 3. Then cross it

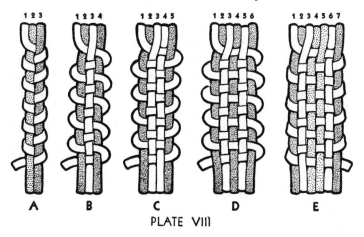

PLATE VIII

over No. 3 and bring it back to the left under No. 2.
Keep weaving the strand from left to right and then back
from right to left.

B. *Four strands.* Bring the outer left strand, No 1 in
Figure B, to the right over No. 2, under No. 3, and over
No. 4. Bring it back under No. 4, over No. 3, and under
No. 2.

C. *Five strands.* Bring the outer left strand, No. 1 in
Figure C, over No. 2, under No. 3, over No. 4, and under
No. 5. Bring it back over No. 5, under No. 4, over No.
3, and under No. 2.

D. *Six strands.* Bring the outer left strand, No. 1 in

Figure D, over No. 2, under No. 3, over No. 4, under No. 5, and over No. 6. Bring it back under No. 6, over No. 5, under No. 4, over No. 3, and under No. 2.

E. *Seven strands.* Bring the outer left strand, No. 1 in Figure E, over No. 2, under No. 3, over No. 4, under No. 5, over No. 6, and under No. 7. Bring it back over No. 7, under No. 6, over No. 5, under No. 4, over No. 3, and under No. 2.

This same process may be used with any number of vertical strands. With odd numbers of strands, the cross strand will always be brought under the outer right strand at the end of the crossing to the right and must therefore be brought over the strand in returning to the left; with even numbers of strands, the cross strand will always be brought over the last vertical strand at the right and must be brought under it, in returning to the left.

Two Strands Woven across Together

Two strands may be used together as a double strand

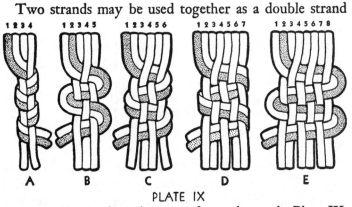

PLATE IX

to weave across the other strands, as shown in Plate IX. The general directions for weaving single strands across apply also to the weaving of double strands. Either the two outer left or the two outer right strands may be used as the working strands. They may be folded over the outer left and right vertical strands, as in Figures A, C, and D, or they may be kept flat, as in Figures B and E.

A. *Four strands.* Bring strands Nos. 1 and 2 in Figure A together over No. 3 and under No. 4. Then bring them over No. 4 and back to the left under No. 3.

B. *Five strands.* Bring strands Nos. 1 and 2 in Figure B together over No. 3, under No. 4, and over No. 5. Then pass them under No. 5 and back to the left over No. 4 and under No. 3.

C. *Six strands.* Bring strands Nos. 1 and 2 in Figure C together over No. 3, under No. 4, over No. 5, and under No. 6. Then bring them back to the left over No. 6, under No. 5, over No. 4, and under No. 3.

D. *Seven strands.* Bring strands Nos. 1 and 2 in Figure D together over No. 3, under No. 4, over No. 5, under No. 6, and over No. 7. Bring them back to the left, under No. 7, over No. 6, under No. 5, over No. 4, and under No. 3.

E. *Eight strands.* (Figure E.) For eight strands or any even number of strands, the process is the same as for six strands.

For nine or other odd numbers of strands the process is the same as for five and seven strands.

Three Strands Woven across Together

Three strands may be used together as a triple strand to weave across the other strands, as shown in Plate X. They may be folded over the outer vertical strands, as in Figures A and C, or kept flat, as in Figures B and D.

A. *Five strands.* Bring strands Nos. 1, 2, and 3 in Figures A together over No. 4, and under No. 5. Cross them over No. 5 and bring them back to the left under No. 4.

B. *Six strands.* Bring strands Nos. 1, 2, and 3 in Figure

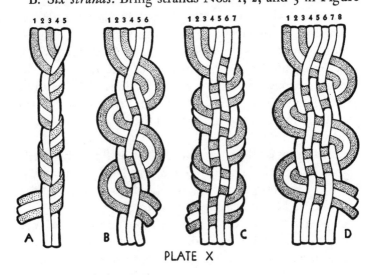

PLATE X

B together over No. 4, under No. 5, and over No. 6. Pass them under No. 6 and bring them back to the left over No. 5 and under No. 4.

The same process may be applied to any number of strands, using either the three outer left or the three outer right strands together to weave across the others. Figure C shows the effect with seven strands and Figure D, with eight strands.

Two Strands Woven across Alternately

Instead of two strands' being used together as a double strand, they may be woven alternately across one or more vertical strands, as shown in Plate XI. In this method usually the outer left strand and the outer right strand are used as the working strands.

A. *Three strands.* Bring the outer left strand, No. 1 in Figure A, over No. 2 and under No. 3 and leave it in horizontal position at the right. Then bring the outer right strand, No. 3, under No. 2 and leave it horizontal

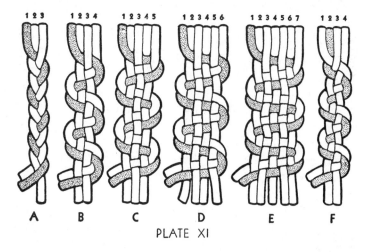

PLATE XI

at the left. Bring No. 1 back to the left over No. 2. Then bring No. 3, the upper horizontal strand at the left, over the lower horizontal, No. 1, and back to the right under No. 2. Bring No. 1 to the right over No. 2. At the right, bring No. 3 over No. 1, and then to the left under No. 2. Bring No. 1 to the left over No. 2. Continue by repeating these steps.

B. *Four strands.* Bring the outer left strand, No. 1 in Figure B, over No. 2, under No. 3, and over No. 4, leaving it in horizontal position at the right. Bring the outer right strand, No. 4, to the left over No. 3 and under No. 2, leaving it in horizontal position at the left. Then bring

No. 1 to the left under No. 3 and over No. 2, leaving it in horizontal position at the left. Bring No. 4, the upper of the left horizontal strands, over No. 1 and back to the right under No. 2 and over No. 3. Bring No. 1 to the right over No. 2 and under No. 3. Continue by repeating these steps.

C. *Five strands.* Bring the outer left strand, No. 1 in Figure C, over No. 2, under No. 3, over No. 4, and under No. 5, leaving it in horizontal position at the right. Then bring the outer right strand, No. 5, to the left under No. 4, over No. 3, and under No. 2. Bring No. 1 to the left over No. 4, under No. 3, and over No. 2. Bring No. 5, the upper of the horizontal strands at the left, across No. 1 and back to the right under No. 2, over No. 3, and under No. 4. Bring No. 1 to the right over No. 2, under No. 3, and over No. 4. Continue by repeating these steps.

Figures D and E show the process for six and seven strands respectively.

Six, eight, and all other even numbers of strands are done as in the directions for four strands. The upper horizontal strand is passed behind the lower horizontal when working on one side of the braid; it is passed over the lower horizontal strand when working at the other side. If you start with the outer left strand first, as in the directions given, the back crossing will take place on the right side and the over crossing, on the left. If you start with the outer right strand, which is also possible, the back crossing will take place on the left side and the front crossing on the right.

Seven, nine, eleven, and all odd numbers of strands are done as in the directions for three and five strands—the upper horizontal strand is crossed over the lower horizontal on both sides of the work.

Instead of the outer left and the outer right strands' being used, as in the preceding method, two neighboring strands, e. g. No. 1 and No. 2 or No. 3 and No. 4, may be used to weave across alternately.

Four strands. Bring the outer left strand, No. 1 in Figure F, to the right over No. 2, under No. 3, and over No. 4, leaving it in horizontal position at the right. Then bring No. 2 over No. 3 and under No. 4, leaving it in horizontal position at the right. Pass the upper horizontal strand, No. 1 at the right, behind No. 2, then to the left over No. 4 and under No. 3. Then bring No. 2 to the left, under No. 4 and over No. 3. The strands at the left are now in the same position as described for the preceding method, Figure B, and the work is continued in the same way.

Two neighboring strands may be similarly woven alternately across higher numbers of strands.

Three Strands Woven across Successively

Three strands may be woven successively across one or more vertical strands, as shown in Plate XII.

A. *Four strands.* Bring the outer left strand, No. 1 in Figure A, over No. 2, under No. 3, and over No. 4, leaving it in horizontal position at the right. Then bring No. 2 over No. 3 and under No. 4, leaving it in horizontal position. Bring No. 3 over No. 4, leaving it in horizontal position. Keep No. 4 straight.

Bring No. 1, the upper of the horizontal strands, down behind No. 2, over No. 3, and then to the left under No. 4, leaving it in horizontal position at the left. Then bring No. 2, now the top horizontal, down behind No. 3 and then to the left over No. 4. Bring No. 3 to the left under

No. 4. Strands Nos. 1, 2, and 3 are now all in horizontal position at the left of No. 4. Bring the top horizontal, No. 1 down over No. 2, pass it behind No. 3 and then to the right over No. 4. Bring No. 2 down over No. 3 and then to the right under No. 4. Bring No. 3 over No. 4

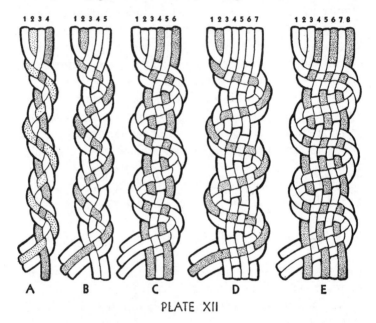

PLATE XII

to the right. The three strands are now all in horizontal position at the right, as they were before; therefore repeat the operation already described.

B. *Five strands.* Bring the outer left strand No. 1 in Figure B, over No. 2, under No. 3, over No. 4, and under No. 5, leaving it in horizontal position at the right. Then bring No. 2 over No. 3, under No. 4, and over No. 5, leaving it in horizontal position at the right. Bring No. 3 over No. 4 and under No. 5, out to the right. Strands

Nos. 1, 2, and 3 are now at the right of Nos. 4 and 5, which are kept straight. Bring the top horizontal strand, No. 1, down over No. 2, under No. 3, and then to the left over No. 5 and under No. 4, leaving it in horizontal position at the left. Bring No. 2 down over No. 3 and then to the left, under No. 5 and over No. 4. Bring No. 3 to the left over No. 5 and under No. 4. The three strands are now at the left in horizontal position. Bring the upper horizontal, No. 1, down over No. 2, under No. 3, and then to the right over No. 4 and under No. 5. Bring No. 2 down over No. 3, and then to the right under No. 4 and over No. 5. Bring No. 3 to the right over No. 4 and under No. 5. Continue by repeating these steps on the right and on the left.

C. *Six strands* (Figure C), *eight strands* (Figure E), and all other even numbers of strands. Bring the strands Nos. 1, 2, and 3 successively across the other strands, as described for four strands. The braiding down on the right and left sides will be different, as it was for four strands. The upper horizontal will be brought down behind the second horizontal for the first step on the side when working at the right of the vertical strands; it will be brought down over the second horizontal when working at the left.

D. *Seven strands* (Figure D), and all odd numbers of strands. The weaving of the three strands across the other vertical strands will be the same as already directed. The braiding down on the sides will be the same both on the right and on the left of the vertical strands, as it was for five strands, i. e., the top horizontal will always be brought down over the second horizontal for the first step at the sides.

Four Strands Woven across Successively

Four strands may be woven successively across **one or** more vertical strands, as shown in Plate XIII.

A. *Five strands.* Bring the outer left strand, No. 1 in Figure A, over No. 2, under No. 3, over No. 4, and under

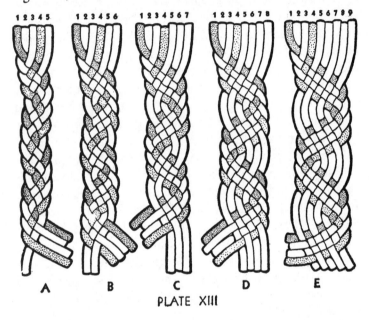

PLATE XIII

No. 5, leaving it in horizontal position at the right. Bring No. 2 over No. 3, under No. 4, and over No. 5, leaving it in horizontal position. Bring No. 3 over No. 4 and under No. 5, leaving it in horizontal position. Bring No. 4 over No. 5. The four strands Nos. 1, 2, 3, and 4 are now at the right of No. 5, which is kept straight. Bring the top horizontal strand, No. 1, down over No. 2, behind No. 3, over No. 4, and then to the left under No. 5. Bring No. 2 down over No. 3, behind No. 4, and then to the left over No.

5. Bring No. 3 down over No. 4, and then to the left under No. 5. Bring No. 4 to the left over No. 5. The horizontal strands are now at the left in the same position as they were at the right and the work is done in the same way.

B. *Six strands.* Bring the outer left strand, No. 1 in Figure B, over No. 2, under No. 3, over No. 4, under No. 5, and over No. 6, leaving it in horizontal position at the right. Bring No. 2 over No. 3, under No. 4, over No. 5, and under No. 6, leaving it in horizontal position. Bring No. 3 over No. 4, under No. 5, and over No. 6, leaving it in horizontal position. Bring No. 4 over No. 5 and under No. 6, leaving it in horizontal position. The four strands, Nos. 1, 2, 3, and 4, are now at the right of Nos. 5 and 6, which are kept straight. Bring the upper horizontal strand, No. 1, down behind No. 2, over No. 3, under No. 4, and then to the left over No. 6 and under No. 5. Bring the next horizontal strand, No. 2, down behind No. 3, over No. 4, and then to the left, under No. 6 and over No. 5. Bring No. 3 down behind No. 4 and then to the left, over No. 6 and under No. 5. The four strands are now in horizontal position at the left. Bring No. 1 down over No. 2, under No. 3, over No. 4 and then to the right, under No. 5 and over No. 6. Bring the next horizontal, No. 2, over No. 3, under No. 4, and then to the right, over No. 5 and under No. 6. Bring No. 4 to the right over No. 5 and under No. 6. The horizontal strands are now again at the right. Continue by repeating the processes as already directed.

For seven, nine, and all odd numbers of strands follow the directions given under five strands. For eight, ten, and all even numbers of strands follow the directions given under six strands.

Five Strands Woven across Successively

If the braiding material is narrow, five or more strands may be woven successively across one or more vertical strands. The steps are similar to the directions which have been given for weaving three or four strands across suc-

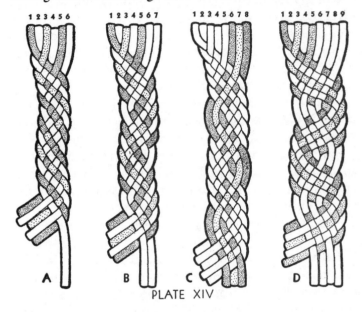

PLATE XIV

cessively. The weaving of five strands across is shown in Plate XIV.

Three Strands Woven across to a Point on Each Side

Three strands may be woven across one or more vertical strands and brought to a point on each side.

A. *Four strands.* The first steps in this method of braiding, shown in Plate XV, are the same as the directions previously given for weaving three strands across vertical strands. First, bring the outer left strand, No. 1 in Figure A, over No. 2, under No. 3, and over No. 4, leaving it in horizontal position at the right. Then bring No. 2 over No. 3 and under No. 4, leaving it in horizontal position. Bring No. 3 over No. 4, leaving it in horizontal position. The three cross strands are now in horizontal position at the right of strand No. 4, which is

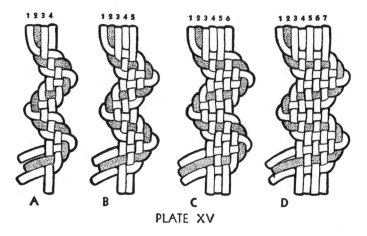

PLATE XV

kept vertical. Bring the upper horizontal strand, No. 1, behind No. 2 and over No. 3 and leave it in vertical position beside No. 4. Bring No. 2 behind No. 3 and leave it in vertical position beside No. 1. No. 3 is now the remaining cross strand. Fold No. 3 under No. 2 horizontally, and then bring it to the left over No. 1 and under No. 4, leaving it horizontal at the left of No. 4. In folding No. 3 under No. 2, if it is folded directly back, it will be wrong-side up when brought to the left; it can be kept right-side up, if desired, by making a little flat loop instead of a sharp crossing under No. 2. This also applies to the other cross strands. Bring No. 2, which is the outer right vertical, horizontally under No. 1 and over No. 4, leaving it horizontal at the left of No. 4. Bring No. 1 under No. 4 into horizontal position at the left. The three cross strands are now in horizontal position at the left of No. 4, No. 3 being the upper horizontal. Bring No. 3 down vertically over No. 2 and behind No. 1. Bring No. 2 down vertically over No. 1. Then fold No. 1 horizontally over No. 2 and bring it to the right under No. 3 and over No. 4. Bring No. 2 to the right over No. 3 and under No. 4. Bring No. 3 to the right over No. 4. Continue in the same way, following the directions given for the process first on the right and then on the left of No. 4, which is kept vertical throughout.

B. *Five strands.* Bring the outer left strand, No. 1 in Figure B, over No. 2, under No. 3, over No. 4 and, under No. 5, leaving it in horizontal position at the right. Bring No. 2 over No. 3, under No. 4, and over No. 5, leaving it in horizontal position. Bring No. 3 over No. 4 and under No. 5, leaving it in horizontal position. Strands Nos. 1, 2, and 3 are now in horizontal position at the right of Nos. 4 and 5, which are kept vertical. Bring the top horizontal, No. 1, down vertically over No. 2 and behind No. 3. Bring No. 2 down vertically over No. 3. No. 3 is now the remaining horizontal strand. Fold No. 3 back horizontally over No. 2, then bring it to the left under No. 1, over No. 5, and under No. 4. Bring No. 2 back horizontally over No. 1, under No. 5, and over No. 4. Bring No. 1 back horizontally over No. 5 and under No. 4. The three cross strands are now in horizontal position at the left of Nos. 4 and 5, No. 3 being the upper horizontal. Bring No. 3 down vertically over No. 2 and behind No. 1. Bring No. 2 down over No. 1. No. 1 is now the remaining horizontal strand. Fold No. 1 horizontally over No. 2, then bring it to the right under No. 3, over No. 4, and under No. 5. Bring No. 2 to the right over No. 3, under No. 4, and over No. 5. Bring No. 3 to the right over No. 4 and under No. 5. The three cross strands are now at the right of Nos. 4 and 5 and the process already described is repeated.

C. *Six strands.* Bring the outer left strand, No. 1 in Figure C, over No. 2, under No. 3, over No. 4, under No. 5, and over No. 6, leaving it in horizontal position at the right. Bring No. 2 over No. 3, under No. 4, over No. 5, and under No. 6, leaving it in horizontal position. Bring No. 3 over No. 4, under No. 5, and over No. 6, leaving it in horizontal position. The three cross strands are now at the right of Nos. 4, 5, and 6, which are kept vertical. Bring the top horizontal, No. 1, down vertically behind No. 2 and over No. 3. Bring No. 2 down vertically behind No. 3. Fold No. 3 horizontally under No. 2 and bring it to the left over No. 1, under No. 6, over No. 5, and under No. 4. Bring No. 2 to the left under No. 1, over No. 6, under No. 5, and over No. 4. Bring No. 1 to the left under No. 6, over No. 5, and under No. 4. The three cross strands are now at the left of Nos. 4, 5, and 6. No. 3 is the upper horizontal strand. Bring No. 3 down vertically over No. 2 and behind No. 1. Bring No. 2 down over No. 1. No. 1 is now the remaining horizontal strand. Fold No. 1 horizontally over No. 2 and bring it to the right under No. 3, over No. 4, under No. 5, and over No. 6. Bring No. 2 to the right over No. 3, under No. 4, over No. 5, and under No. 6. Bring No. 3 to the right over No. 4, under No. 5, and over No. 6. The three cross strands are now at the right in the same position as before and the process already described is repeated.

Three cross strands may be woven across any number of vertical strands by this method. When there is an even total number of strands—eight, ten, twelve, etc. —there will be an odd number of vertical strands. In these cases, the first step with each horizontal strand at the right will be to bring it down behind the next strand; on the left, the first step with each horizontal strand will be to bring it over the next strand. When there is an odd total number of strands—seven, nine, eleven, etc.—there will be an even number of vertical strands. In these cases, the first step with each horizontal strand both on the right and on the left will be to bring it down over the next strand.

Four Strands Woven across to a Point on Each Side

Four strands may be woven across one or more vertical strands and brought to a point on each side, as shown in Plate XVI.

A. *Five strands.* Bring the outer left strand, No. 1 of Figure A, over No. 2, under No. 3, over No. 4, and under No. 5, leaving it in horizontal position at the right. Bring No. 2 over No. 3, under No. 4, and over No. 5, leaving it in horizontal position. Bring No. 3 over No. 4 and under No. 5, leaving it in horizontal position. Bring No. 4 over No. 5. The four cross strands are now in horizontal position at the right of No. 5, which is kept vertical. Bring the upper horizontal, No. 1, down vertically over No. 2, behind No. 3, and over No. 4. Bring No. 2 down vertically over No. 3 and behind No. 4. Bring No. 3 down over No. 4. No. 4 is now the remaining horizontal strand. Fold No. 4 horizontally over No. 3, then bring it to the left under No. 2, over No. 1, and under No. 5. Bring No. 3 to the left over No. 2, under No. 1, and over No. 5. Bring No. 2 to the left over No. 1 and under No. 5. Bring No. 1 to the left over No. 5. The four cross strands are now in horizontal position at the left of No. 5. No. 4 is the upper horizontal. Bring No. 4

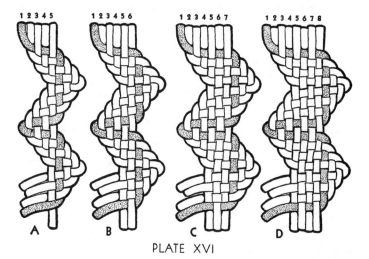

PLATE XVI

down vertically over No. 3, behind No. 2, and over No. 1. Bring No. 3 down vertically over No. 2 and behind No. 1. Bring No. 2 down over No. 1. No. 1 is now the remaining horizontal strand. Fold No. 1 horizontally over No. 2, then bring it to the right under No. 3, over No. 4, and under No. 5. Bring No. 2 to the right over No. 3, under No. 4, and over No. 5. Bring No. 3 to the right over No. 4 and under No. 5. Bring No. 4 to the right over No. 5. The four cross strands are now at the right in the same position as they were before and the process previously described is repeated.

B. *Six strands.* Bring the outer left strand, No. 1 of Figure B, over No. 2, under No. 3, over No. 4, under

No. 5, and over No. 6, leaving it in horizontal position at the right. Bring No. 2 over No. 3, under No. 4, over No. 5, and under No. 6, leaving it in horizontal position. Bring No. 3 over No. 4, under No. 5, and over No. 6, leaving it in horizontal position. Bring No. 4 over No. 5 and under No. 6, leaving it in horizontal position. The four cross strands are now in horizontal position at the right of Nos. 5 and 6, which are kept vertical. Bring the upper horizontal, No. 1, down vertically behind No. 2, over No. 3, and behind No. 4. Bring No. 2 down vertically behind No. 3 and over No. 4. Bring No. 3 down behind No. 4. No. 4 is now the remaining horizontal strand. Fold No. 4 horizontally under No. 3, then bring it to the left over No. 2, under No. 1, over No. 6, and under No. 5. Bring No. 3 to the left under No. 2, over No. 1, under No. 6, and over No. 5. Bring No. 2 to the left under No. 1, over No. 6, and under No. 5. Bring No. 1 to the left under No. 6 and over No. 5. The four cross strands are now in horizontal position at the left. Bring No. 4, the upper horizontal, down vertically over No. 3, behind No. 2, and over No. 1. Bring No. 3 down vertically over No. 2 and behind No. 1. Bring No. 2 down over No. 1. No. 1 is now the remaining horizontal strand. Fold No. 1 horizontally over No. 2, then bring it to the right under No. 3, over No. 4, under No. 5, and over No. 6. Bring No. 2 to the right over No. 3, under No. 4, over No. 5, and under No. 6. Bring No. 3 to the right over No. 4, under No. 5, and over No. 6. Bring No. 4 to the right over No. 5 and under No. 6. The four cross strands are now at the right in the same position as they were before and the process previously described is repeated.

When there is an odd total number of strands, there

will be an odd number of vertical strands. In these cases, the work on the right and left of the verticals is the same, always beginning by bringing the upper horizontal down over the second horizontal. When there is an even total number of strands, there will be an even number of

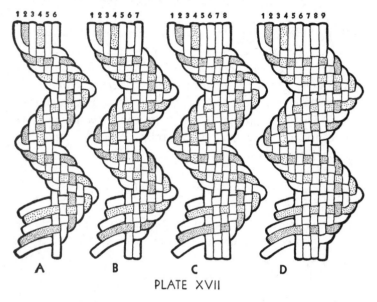

PLATE XVII

vertical strands. In these cases, the work at the right begins by bringing the upper horizontal down behind the second horizontal, whereas at the left it begins by bringing the upper horizontal down over the second one.

Any number of strands may be woven across one, two or more vertical strands in the same way as has been described for weaving three or four strands. The illustrations in Plate XVII show five strands woven across one, two, three, and four vertical strands.

CHAPTER IV

Articles of Flat Braiding

THE articles described in this chapter have been selected as simple and practical illustrations of some of the processes the directions for which have been given in the preceding chapters, and also as suggestions for the use of various braiding materials. Other materials, however, may be quite feasibly substituted and the sizes and shapes may be varied according to the worker's pleasure.

Oval Rug or Mat

Material:

> Any material which, when braided, can be sewed together. The amount of material needed depends upon the thickness of the braiding strands and the size desired for the mat or rug.

Mats and rugs of braids sewed together in round or oval shapes have long been among the commonest and most serviceable uses of braiding. Most familiar are the floor rugs of braided strips of cloth, but the same process may be applied to other materials, as in the use of various braided fibers for small table mats, plant stands, or chair seat pads.

For the making of cloth rugs, any washable material may be used, but cotton and wool should not be combined in the same rug, as they would shrink unevenly when wet. The width of the strips into which the cloth should be cut for the braiding depends upon the weight of the material. Strips of denim should be about $1\frac{1}{4}$ inches wide, while gingham strips should be about $2\frac{1}{2}$ inches. After the strips are cut, fold in the raw edges, then fold the strips in the middle so that the folded strands

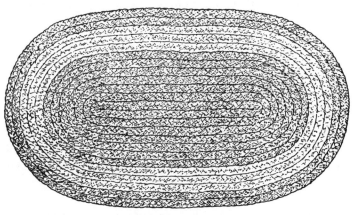

PLATE   XVIII

will be about $\frac{3}{8}$ inch wide. Press the folded strips, if necessary, to flatten them.

To join one strip to another for added length, cut the ends of strips at opposite diagonals and lay one end over the other. Ordinarily do not turn the ends in, as this would make the join too bulky. Using strong thread, sew with running stitches in zigzag lines back and forth across the join, being careful to take in the raw edges with the stitches.

The braid for a rug may be made either with three strands (Plate I, Figure A) or four strands (Plate III, Figure A); four-strand braiding is usually preferable.

In making a rug, the entire length of braid may be one continuous strip, coiled round and round in either circular or oval rows, or each round or oval may be finished off separately, as in the rug illustrated in Plate XVIII. The latter method is especially desirable if there are to be rounds of differing colors.

Any oval mat should be started with a straight "keel," the length of which should be equal to the difference between the intended length and width of the finished rug. A rug, for instance, which is to be 40 inches long and 22 inches wide must be started with a keel 18 inches long. In measuring the keel, do not include the thickness of the braid at either end. If you are to use a continuous length of braid for the rug, the keel is a single uncut end of the braid of the length desired. The braid is then sewed entirely around the keel so that the keel is in a straight line in the middle of the first oval. If each oval is to be finished off, as in the illustration, the keel is the straight seam which joins the two sides of the braid when it is formed into the first oval. In either method, be very careful to allow just enough curvature at both ends of the oval so that the braid will lie absolutely flat. It is best to pin the work in position with strong pins before you begin to sew it.

Use heavy linen carpet thread and a strong needle for sewing. Make flat stitches from the outside loops of one round of braid through the outside loops of the adjoining round and so place your stitches that the thread will be concealed in the cloth.

If the rounds are to be finished off each time, after the first oval has been nearly all sewed, cut off the two ends of the braid at opposite diagonals and join the strands in the manner already described, sewing them down first on the top and then on the bottom of the rug. Start the next round at any point at a distance from the join just made and plan succeeding rows similarly, so that the joins, being at different places in the rug, will not be conspicuous.

Sandals of Tropical Fiber

MATERIALS:

> 4 lengths of tropical fiber, all of same color or in two contrasting colors, each length about 250 inches for a pair of size 6 sandals.
>
> I pair inner soles
>
> Large needle and linen thread

For each sandal, shown in Plate XIX, use two of the 250 inch lengths. Tie both lengths together at their centers with a piece of string and, with the same string, attach them to a steady object. The two lengths form four strands, each of about 125 inches. Braid by the method of four-strand braiding described on page 10. Make the braiding firm but do not pull it too tight. Continue for the entire length of the strands, making a braid about 100 inches long. The braid is then to be sewed to the inner sole.

The inner sole should be firm but of material soft enough to sew through and it should be about one-half inch narrower than the width desired for the sandal. Sew the braid first on the bottom of the sole. Start at the instep and sew the braid on flat around the edge, allowing it to project a little (about the thickness of one strand) beyond the edge. Sew through the sole, keeping the stitches in line with the strands, so that they will sink in and be concealed. When you have sewed once around the sole and are to cross over the end with which you started, open the under strands as flat as possible so that they will not form a bulky lump as you sew the braid over them. Then continue sewing on the braid, without cutting it, making the second row next to the outside row and very close to it, and so on to the center of the sole. At the center you may have to pull the braid to make it thinner or spread it, as the case may be, to fill the remaining space. Then cut

PLATE XIX

off the braid, leaving just enough of an end so that it can be worked under the preceding row of braiding. You will have to cut one or two stitches of the preceding row. Spread the ends of the braid, insert them under the other braid, and sew them down as flat as possible.

Turn the sandal over and sew the braid on the top in the same way.

For the straps, cut two strips of the braid of the desired length. As shown in the sandal illustrated, one end of each strap is inserted at the side of the heel, the strap is carried around the heel and then across the sandal to a point about half way between the tip of the sandal and the instep, where the other end is inserted. The two straps cross at the back of the sandal and form a little hold for the heel. The two straps may, if preferred, be crossed over each other at the front of the sandal, without being carried around the heel. When you have decided on the points where you wish to insert the ends of the straps, cut one or two stitches in the last row of braiding at these points, spread the ends of the straps flat, insert them in the openings you have made for them, and sew them in securely. Sew the straps together at the point where they cross. Then sew all around the edge of the sandal to close the braids of the top and bottom securely together.

Raffia Hat

MATERIALS:
> 6 oz. to 8 oz. raffia
> I large-eyed needle

Raffia, which is obtained from the leaves of the raffia palm, native to Madagascar, is an excellent, yet very inexpensive material for outing hats. It is easy to work with and extraordinarily durable, though of light weight. Possibly its chief recommendation for outing hats lies in the fact that, in contrast with straw and similar materials, raffia improves when it has been dampened or even wet. Raffia may be obtained either in natural color at about 45 cents a pound or, at about twice that price, in beautiful vegetable-dyed colors, which are water-fast and almost sunfast. It is sold in bundles of strips which average about 1¾ yards in length and vary in width from fine shreds to strips of about ½ inch. Buy only raffia which is dry. Avoid raffia which is sticky or which has a glycerined finish, as this is too heavy for hats, though excellent for baskets and similar articles.

Soak the raffia in water, preferably warm, and work with it wet. Select strips which are of about the same width or use enough strips together for a strand so that all the strands of the braid will be of the same thickness. The braid of the hat shown in Plate XX is $\frac{3}{16}$ inch wide. As you proceed with the braiding strive to keep your braid of uniform width. When you are nearing the end of a strip or if the strand becomes too thin, lay a new strip of raffia on top of the others. Drop ends of strips under the braid if the strand seems too thick, if the strip becomes too short to braid, or if a part of the strip is discolored. Always add the new strips when the strand is brought to the middle of the braid in the braid-

PLATE XX

ing process; do not add strips when the strand is on an outer edge of the braid. There will be many short ends protruding from the top and bottom of the braid as you work; they should be clipped off close with sharp scissors while they are still damp. Pulling the wet braid as you go along will serve to make it even and straight. A hat of the style illustrated requires about 17 yards of braid $\frac{3}{16}$ inch wide. After you have made the entire length of braid, cover it, a section at a time, with a cloth wrung out of water and press it with a hot iron. The pressing will flatten the braid, make it more pliable, and also give the raffia a glossy finish.

The hat may be of any shape you select. It is best to have a hat of the same style as a guide on which to try the work repeatedly; otherwise, try it on your head or the head of the person for whom it is being made. The finished hat can be blocked for about 25 cents, if necessary, so that slight irregularities in the shape or a head-size which is either too large or too small can be easily remedied.

The hat is to be started at the center of the crown. Unbraid the beginning of your length of braid for about 7 inches. Re-braid about one inch, but thin it out abruptly so that it is reduced to about one-half the thickness of the rest of the braid. Lay the remaining unbraided ends as flat as you can on a table and coil the braid in a circle, or if you wish an oval-shaped crown, lay a straight keel, as explained in the directions for oval rugs on page 48. Use narrow strips of wet raffia and a large-eyed darning needle for sewing. Do not use thread, as it will break the raffia and eventually, if not immediately, cut right through it. Make horizontal stitches either through both the braids that are being joined or from the center of one braid to the center of the other. Where the shape is to be kept flat or nearly flat, it is better to sew entirely through the braids.

After you have completed the top of the crown, interrupt your work, while you moisten the short ends which you left at the beginning, thread each strip separately onto your needle, work it through the braids, and clip it off neatly.

Then continue to sew on the rounds of braid for the depth of the crown, testing it frequently to make sure that you are getting the shape as you wish it. In the hat illustrated, the brim is continuous with the crown. If, however, you wish to finish the crown off separately, which is really necessary in a flat-brimmed hat of a sailor shape, cut off the braid about 6 inches longer than you need for finishing the round, un-braid the six-inch end, thin it out as you re-braid for about 2 inches until it is as thin as you can make it. Sew the thinned end to the adjoining row, thread the remaining ends onto your needle, work them into the braid, and clip them off close.

In joining the first round of the brim to the crown, whether the brim is continuous with the crown or separate, hold the crown pointing downward, and sew the round of braid on with over and over, instead of flat stitches. For the second and succeeding rows, change back to flat stitches either through the entire widths of the adjoining braids or through half their widths. The hat illustrated has a brim of uniform width all around. If you wish to make a part of the brim wider than the rest, begin to widen after you have sewed on two or three rounds of the brim. Cut strips of the braid of the proper lengths, sew one of the strips to the last complete row in the position where you wish it, and carry the next round of braid around the insert when you come to it. Then sew on another short strip, and carry the next round of braid around this insert, and so on, until you have added as much extra width as you need.

Finish off the brim in the same way as has been directed for finishing off a crown which is to be separate from the brim.

The hat illustrated can be worn with either side out and the brim can be turned up in whatever way one wishes.

Suede Leather Belt

MATERIALS:

Strip of Suede Leather about 1¼ in. wide and of length required.
Buckle

The belt shown in Plate XXI may be made of suede or any other suitable leather. If a heavier leather, like calf, is used, a leather punch will be needed to make perfora-

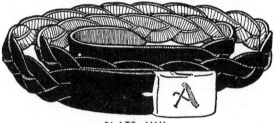

PLATE XXI

tions for securing the buckle to the belt either by hand-stitching or by lacing, whereas suede can be easily sewed by hand or machine.

For the three-strand braided section, which may be merely at the center of the back of the belt or extending nearly the entire length, as illustrated, divide the section very evenly into three parts. Draw the two dividing lines on the back of the leather, and, placing the leather, wrong-side up, on a piece of thick cardboard, cut the lines with a very sharp knife, guided by a metal-edged ruler. Begin at either end of the three strands thus formed and braid them with regular three-strand braiding. Braiding at one end will cause the other end to braid also. To remedy this, keep passing the further end of the belt from front to back through the strands at that end of the braided section. Push the braid up tight, when you are braiding the last part, to enable you to pass the end through. Then even up the braid. The same process is applicable to braids of more than three strands.

For securing the buckle to the belt, pass the square end over the bar of the buckle and stitch by machine or hand. If you sew it by hand, use tailor's buttonhole twist and preferably the cobbler's stitch. This is done by having a needle on each end of the thread and passing one needle through the leather from the top and the other through from the bottom as each stitch is made. If the leather is too heavy to push the needle through, you may use an awl or other sharp-pointed instrument to make perforations for the stitches. Be careful to space them evenly and also make sure that the perforations in the top layer of the leather fall exactly over those in the lower layer.

If you wish to use a buckle with a pin, you should have eyelets in the pointed end of the belt. There are special tools which may be purchased for inserting eyelets, or you may send the belt to an artcraft supply house or to a cobbler to have the eyelets inserted.

Bracelet of Wide Gimp on Metal Band

MATERIALS:
>   Metal band ¾ in. wide
>   About ⅝ yd. coated gimp ¼ in. wide in one color and
>   2¼ yds. in a contrasting color

The method of braiding used in making the bracelet shown in Plate XXII is an adaptation of the process described on page 27 and illustrated in Plate VIII, Figure B.

The metal band is of the same type and should be cut

and fitted together in the same way as the one described on page 79. The measure around the circumference of the bracelet must be evenly divisible into half inches, e. g. 7½, 8, or 8½ inches.

After the band has been formed into a bracelet, cut the shorter length of gimp into three pieces, each about ½ inch longer than the circumference of the bracelet. These three strips are to serve as the stationary strands through which the longer strand is to be woven. Lay the three strips side by side on the bracelet, but have the ends of the strands at different places, not in a straight line

PLATE XXII

across the width of the metal. Hold the three strips on the bracelet at any point with your left thumb and fore-finger, while you weave the longer strip of contrasting gimp over the first top strand, under the second, and over the third. Pull almost the entire length of the strand through. Then pass the strand through the inside of the bracelet, bringing it out beside the row which you have just woven across, and pass it under the first top strand, over the second, and under the third. Pull the work tight. Continue in the same way around the bracelet.

When you come to the points where the ends of the top strands join, be sure that each join is covered by the weaving strand. This can be easily adjusted with the half-inch extra length which you allowed in cutting the strands. When you have completed the weaving entirely around the bracelet, carry the weaving strand over the little end left at the beginning, and, going right over the first row of weaving, work it over, under, and over the top strands, and cut it off at the other side of the bracelet.

CHAPTER V

SOLID BRAIDING

SOLID braiding is used to provide strength or to give an attractive cord effect. The braiding may be done around a central core of the same material as the braiding strands or of any strong cord to give it extra re-enforcement, or it may be done without any core.

Any regular braiding material may be used provided it is strong, as the work must be pulled tight. The material must, therefore, be such that the strands will not break easily. The illustrations show braiding done with coated gimp, which is an excellent material for the processes. It is described on page 78.

Round Braiding

The most common form of solid braiding is "round braiding," which may be made with four, six, or eight strands. The round braiding may be used to continue after a length of flat braiding of the same number of strands; it may be made with the required number of independent strands; or it may be made with two, three, or four lengths of braiding material passed through a clip, over the bar of a belt buckle, or otherwise divided so that each length makes two strands. If the round braiding is to follow flat braiding, stop the work when the strands are arranged with the same number on both sides of the center and secure the work to a vise or other steady object. If you are starting with new strands, arrange them in order, side by side, and make sure that all strands are right-side up, if the material has a right side and a wrong side. In the illustrations the strands were secured between folded gummed paper, as was suggested for flat braiding on page 4.

Four-strand. Bring the second strand from the left, No. 2 in Figure A of Plate XXIII, across No. 3 and pass No. 1

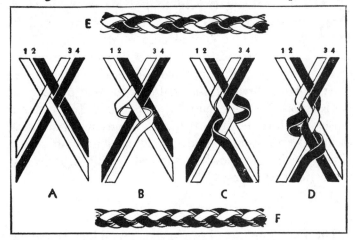

PLATE XXIII

under No. 3. Bring No. 4 over No. 2 and under No. 1. The two left strands have thus been brought to the right and the two right strands, to the left. You have formed a little diamond, with No. 3 the outer left strand and No. 4 next to it; No. 2, the outer right strand and No. 1 next to it. This first weaving of the strands is the preliminary step before you start round braiding.

In the process of round braiding, the braiding strand is passed across the back, out on the opposite side, and then brought across the front, and returned to the side from which it started. The first strand to be used in starting four-strand round braiding from your preliminary interwoven strands must be an outer left or right strand which crosses over, not under. In the arrangement shown, the outer left is an over strand. (If you had crossed your strands by passing No. 3 over No. 2 in the start, which would also have been possible, the outer right would be an over strand and would be used first in starting the round braiding.)

Bring the outer left strand, No. 3, across the back, guiding it with your left forefinger so that you will not twist it, and push it out between the right strands, No. 2 and No. 1. Cross it over No. 1 and bring it back to the left next to No. 4. (Figure B.) Next pass the outer right strand, No. 2, across the back (it will be a little loose), guiding it with your right forefinger and push it out between the left strands, No. 4 and No. 3, then cross it over No. 3 so that it is back at the right next to No. 1. (Figure C.) Then pass the outer left strand, which is now No. 4, across the back and out between No. 1 and No. 2, cross it over No. 2 and back to the left. (Figure D.) Pull the work up tight. To continue: pass the outer right strand across the back, bring it out between the two left strands, then cross it over the lower one and back to the right. Then pass the outer left strand across the back, bring it out between the two right strands, cross it over the lower one and out to the left. As you continue, strands No. 3 and No. 4 are always brought back to the left, and strands No. 2 and No. 1 are always brought back to the right, since the working strands must always be brought back to the side where they were in the little diamond with which the braiding started. Be careful always to keep the strands right-side up.

If you have to leave your work or get confused as to

which outer strand is the next one to use, it will help you to notice the crossing of the two strands in the front of your work. If the upper strand in the crossing goes to the left, the next strand to use must be the outer right one, and vice versa.

If your work becomes unbraided so that the position of the strands is not clear, select any point of crossing in the last firm section of the braid. Pull one of these cross strands out either to the right or to the left, according to the direction in which it slants. If there is a right and wrong side to your material, the crossing strands must be right-side up. Then take the strand that crossed this one, either under or over, before you loosened it and draw it out in the other direction. Work your left forefinger in under the crossing; hold the crossing with your thumb and forefinger while you draw out the other two strands so that there is one on each side parallel to and above each of the two strands you drew out. Then examine the crossing of the strands as explained above, to determine which outer strand you must use first in continuing your work.

Different pattern effects are obtainable by using two contrasting colors, two of the strands being of a darker color and the other two of a lighter color. (1) If the strands are arranged so that the colors are separated with one light and one dark on each side in any order (e. g. No. 1 and No. 3 light, and No. 2 and No. 4 dark, or vice versa; or No. 1 and No. 4 dark, and No. 2 and No. 3 light, or vice versa), the two colors will alternate diagonally around the braid, as shown in Figure E. (2) If the strands are arranged with the same colors together (e. g. No. 1 and No. 2 light, No. 3 and No. 4 dark, or vice versa), the colors will alternate in vertical stripes down the braid, as shown in Figure F.

Six Strands. (Plate XXIV.) Arrange the strands and secure the ends as directed for four-strand round braiding. Bring strand No. 3 over No. 4, under No. 5, and over No. 6. Then weave the other strands No. 2 and No. 1 over or under, as the case may be, Nos. 4, 5, and 6 until you have strands Nos. 1, 2, and 3 at the right, and strands Nos. 4, 5, and 6 at the left. (Figure A.)

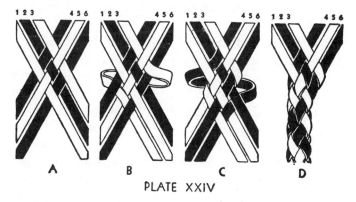

PLATE XXIV

Start the round braiding with the outer right or left strand which is an over strand. In the crossing of the strands as just directed the upper right strand, No. 3, is an over strand. Pass this strand across the back, guiding it with your right forefinger to keep it from twisting, bring it up between Nos. 4 and 5 at the left, then cross it over No. 5, pass it under No. 6, and back to the right. (Figure B.) Then pass the outer left strand, No. 4, across the back, bring it up between Nos. 1 and 2, cross it over No. 1, pass it under No. 3, and back to the left. (Figure C.)

Continue by passing the upper strand, first the outer

right and then the outer left, across the back, bringing it out on the opposite side between the second and third strands from the bottom, then passing it over the second strand and under the bottom strand, and back to the side from which it started. Pull the work up tight every time a working strand has been brought back to the side from which it started.

The arrangement of the colors as in Figure A will produce a braid with the effect shown in Figure D, but various other effects can be procured by different arrangements.

Eight Strands. (Plate XXV.) Arrange the strands and secure the ends. Bring strand No. 4 over No. 5, under No. 6, over No. 7 and under No. 8. Then weave strands Nos. 3, 2, and 1 over and under Nos. 5, 6, 7, and 8 until Nos. 1, 2, 3, and 4 are at the right and Nos. 5, 6, 7, and 8 are at the left. (Figure A.)

Start the round braiding with the outer right strand, No. 4, which is an under strand. In any round braiding, the outer strand with which you start must be one, which, when it is brought across the back and out on the opposite side, will cross over the strand below it. In four-strand or six-strand round braiding, the outer strand which will fill this requirement is one which is an over strand in the interwoven diamond, but in eight-strand round braiding, the outer strand with which you are to start must be an under strand in the diamond.

Pass strand No. 4 across the back and bring it out at the left between the second and third strands from the bottom, No. 6 and No. 7, pass it over No. 7, then under No. 8, and back to the right. (Figure B.) Then pass the upper left strand, No. 5, across the back, bring it out at the right between the second and third strands from the bottom, No. 2 and No. 1, pass it over No. 1, then under No. 4, and back to the left. (Figure C.) Continue in the same way. Be careful not to twist the strands and pull the work up tight every time after a working strand has been brought back to the side from which it started. Figure **D**

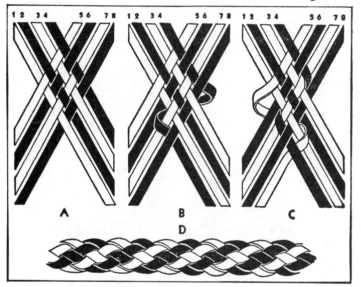

PLATE XXV

shows the effect obtained in the finished braid when the strands have been arranged as in Figure A.

Round Braiding Attached to a Clip or over a Band

If you wish to make a round braid attached to a clip, as for a dog leash, or to braid over a band as for a bracelet (see pages 84 and 78), each length of the gimp or other braiding material should be long enough to make two strands, when it is passed through the clip or around the band.

When the lengths are passed through a clip, it is helpful, in starting the work, to lay a narrow strip of cardboard over the strands and the clip, until you get the
strands in their interwoven positions, as directed previously as the preliminary step in round braiding. The cardboard can be snipped with scissors and easily removed

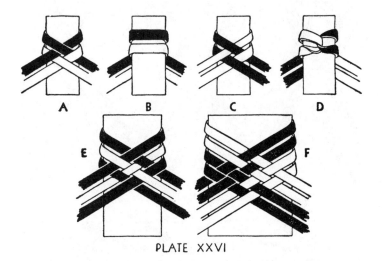

A   B   C   D

E   F

PLATE XXVI

when the braiding is started. If you are braiding around a
flat band, the cardboard is not needed. Figure A of Plate
XXVI shows two lengths of gimp making four strands
on the front of the cardboard or flat band. (The clip is
not shown in the illustration.) Figure B shows the position of the strands on the back. If two lengths of different
colors are used, there will be one strand of each color at
the left and at the right. If you wish both strands on each
side to be of the same color, as in Figure C, you must loop
the two lengths of your braiding material through each
other at the back of the cardboard, as shown in Figure D.

Be sure that you bring the strands right side up across the front. Figure E shows the arrangement for six strands; Figure F, for eight strands.

After you have interwoven the strands, proceed with the round braiding according to the directions which have already been given. If you have inserted the cardboard, clip it and remove it when you start the braiding. If the braiding is over a flat band, which is to be kept in the work, pass the braiding strand across the back of the band and up on the opposite side, then bring it across the top of the band, weaving it over and under the other strands, back to the side from which it started. The process is more fully described in the directions for the bracelet on page 80.

Three-Strand Solid Braiding

In all the preceding methods of braiding, the ends of the strands have been secured in some manner to a steady object and you have worked toward you. In the following methods you must hold the ends of the strands or the length already braided between your left thumb and forefinger and build the braid upward in a vertical position.

Tie the ends of the three strands together and hold them upright between your left thumb and forefinger, or, if you are continuing after a three-strand flat braid, let the completed braid hang down between your thumb and forefinger so that the unused lengths are upward. Have all the strands either right-side up or wrong-side up. In this braiding process, the strands will be right-side up in one row and wrong-side up in the next row. Arrange the strands so that one comes to the front over your thumb, one goes to the right, and the third one goes to the left, as shown in Figure A of Plate XXVII.

Pass the front strand, No. 1 in Figure A, to the right over strand No. 2 but leave a little loop of No. 1 in front and hold the loop under your thumb. (Figures B and C.) Strand No. 1 will lie between the right strand, No. 2, and the left strand, No. 3. Pass No. 2 to the left over both No. 1 and No. 3. (Figure D.) Then bring No. 3 to the front over No. 2 and put it through the loop of No. 1

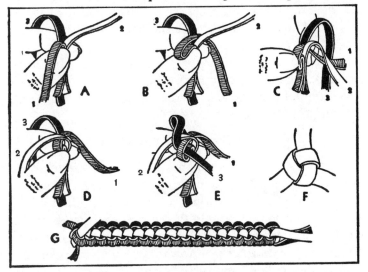

PLATE XXVII

which you have been holding with your thumb. (Figure E.) Pull the three strands so that the work is tight. You will find that you have formed a compact little triangle, as shown in Figure F. The resulting braid, shown in Figure G, will be six-sided. Continue the braiding by repeating these steps. Be careful not to twist the strands during the work.

To end off the braid. In the last row of work the strands must be right-side up. If, therefore, they are wrong-side up when you wish to stop, either add another row or pull out one row so that they will be right-side up. Cut off the strands, leaving ends about the length across the top of the triangle. Make the ends pointed and, using an awl, tuck each end into the braid under the last row.

Spiral Braiding with Four Strands

Spiral braiding with four strands may be done with four tied strands or it may follow any kind of four-strand braiding.

Tie the ends of four strands together with a piece of string and hold the tied ends pointing downward between

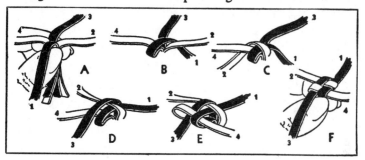

PLATE XXVIII

the thumb and forefinger of the left hand or hold a braided length similarly pointing downward. Allow the lengths of the strands at first to fall over your forefinger. Then separate the strands so that one falls to the front over the thumb, one opposite it over the forefinger, one to the right and the last to the left, as shown in Figure A of Plate XXVIII. If two different colors are used in spiral braiding, they should be arranged in starting so that the front strand over your thumb is of the same color as the back strand over your forefinger, and the left and right strands should be of the other color. If your material has a right and a wrong side, have all the strands with the same side up, either the right or the wrong side. In this type of braiding, one row of work will be right-side up and the next, wrong-side up all through the braiding.

First pass the front strand, No. 1 in Figure A, over the right strand, No. 2, leaving a small loop of No. 1 in front, which you slip under and hold with your left thumb. The front strand, when passed over the right strand will lie between the right strand, No. 2, and the back strand, No. 3. (Figure B.) Then pass the right strand, No. 2, over both strand No. 1 and the back strand, No. 3, so that it lies between No. 3 and the left strand, No. 4. (Figure C.) Bring the back strand over No. 2 and No. 4 so that it lies between the left strand, No. 4, and the little loop of strand No. 1 which you are holding with your thumb. (Figure D.) Then bring the left strand, No. 4, over No. 3, pass it through the little loop, and draw it tight, at the same time tightening the other strands also. (Figure E.) You will find that you have made a little cross-sectioned square with one strand extending from each side. (Figure F.) The little square may be turned with any one of the four sides facing you for the front side. Whichever strand is in front (and in this method it will always be on the left half of the front) is considered the front strand and the work is repeated as already directed. Draw up the little square very tight each time by tightening each strand separately and holding the tightened strands while you pull the others. Be careful not to twist the strands during the work—merely fold them over rather loosely and then tighten them after the square is formed. The strands should be all right-side up in one square and all wrong-side up in the next.

This method of braiding will give a spiral, running across the braid from the upper left to the lower right side, as in the left section of Figure D of Plate XXIX. If the work had been done by starting the front strand to the left, instead of to the right, and then using the left strand, the back strand, and lastly the right strand, in the

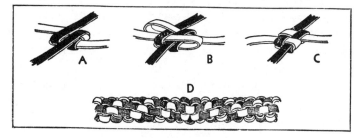

PLATE   XXIX

reverse order from the directions given, you would have a spiral, running from the upper right to the lower left, as in the right section of Figure D. The front strands would then always come on the right half of the front. If the front strand is on the right of the front, it must be crossed over to the left; if it is on the left, it must be crossed over to the right.

Reversing the Spiral

It is often effective to have the spiral run in one direction for part of the braiding and then to reverse it to the other direction. An intermediate step is needed in order to change the position of the front strands, which is necessary to make the spiral change direction.

Turn your work with any side of the little square formed by the last row of braiding toward you. First lay the front strand straight across the square so that it is at the back and bring the back strand straight across to the front. (Figure A of Plate XXIX.) Then weave the right strand over one and under the other of these two cross strands so that it comes out at the left; weave the left strand similarly across so that it comes out at the right. (Figure B.) Pull the work up tight. (Figure C.) Turn toward you any one of the four sides of the little square just made and your front strand is on the other half of the front from where it was originally and is in position to continue the spiral braiding in the opposite direction from your previous spiral.

Spiral braiding may be finished by tucking in the ends as directed for three-strand solid braiding or with a lock knot, described on page 76.

Square Braiding with Four Strands

Square braiding with four strands may be done with four tied strands or it may follow any kind of four-strand braiding.

Arrange the strands in exactly the same way as directed above for spiral braiding and follow the directions for spiral braiding until you have formed the first little square. Square braiding must always be started with this one row of spiral braiding. (See Plate XXX, Figures A, B, C, D, E, F.) Then hold the work with any of the four sides of the little square toward you. Fold the front strand across the top, so that it lies to the back and bring the back strand across the top so that it comes to the front. (Figure G.) Then weave the right strand over and under these two top strands so that it comes to the left. Similarly weave the left strand across the top through the same cross strands over one and under the other. (Figure H.)

You may have to use an awl or similar tool to loosen the top strand for the last step. Draw the strands tight. (Figure I.) Continue in the same way, always laying two opposite strands across the top and then weaving the other strands through them. It will be observed that this is the same

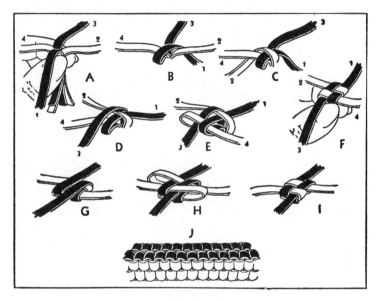

PLATE XXX

process as the step described for reversing the spiral in spiral braiding. Figure J shows the effect obtained by four-strand square braiding.

Six strands and eight strands may be square-braided similarly but the start of the work is too complicated to illustrate.

Square braiding may be ended off by the same methods as directed for spiral braiding on page 72.

Square Braiding with a Finished End

If you wish a four-strand square braid to begin with a finished end, you must use two lengths of the braiding material, each of which becomes two strands. In starting you will find it helpful to fold them, right-side up, across a small square of cardboard, as shown in Figure A¹ of

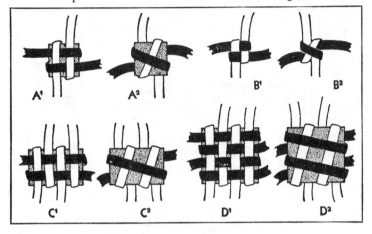

PLATE XXXI

Plate XXXI. Weave the four strands formed by the two lengths over and under each other until you have a little woven square on top of the cardboard. The under side of the cardboard is shown in Figure A². After you have formed the square, snip the cardboard with a pair of scissors and remove it. Then draw the work up tight, as in figure B¹. The back view is shown in Figure B².

The finished square is to be used for the end of the braid. Therefore, hold the work between your left thumb and forefinger, with the finished end down. Lay the front strand over the top to the back and the back strand over the top to the front across the two diagonally crossing strands, to which no attention is paid. Then weave the left and right strands over and under the front and back strands. Continue the square braiding.

Figures C[1] and C[2] show the arrangement of three lengths, making six strands for square braiding on the front and back of the cardboard; figures D[1] and D[2] show the arrangement of four lengths, making eight strands.

Braiding with a Core

A core is a center foundation around which a braid is made. It is inserted to give extra strength to the braid and may be of the same material as the braiding strands or it may be of strong cord, wire or any other suitable material.

A core may be used in any of the forms of solid braiding. It is simply kept in the center of the work and the instructions for the braiding processes are followed just as if the core were not there. Usually the work is pulled up as tightly as possible around the core. The dog leash on page 84, and the bracelet on page 78 show uses of cores in solid braiding.

Lock Knot

A lock knot may be used to end off any kind of four-strand braiding, round, spiral, or square, but it is necessary to have one row of square braiding as a basis. Therefore, unless you have been making a length of square braiding, you must make one row of square braiding with the preliminary row of spiral braiding, as directed on page 72. Do not pull the square tight. The front strand may be either on the left or on the right half of the front; the directions differ accordingly.

(1). *When front strand is on left half of front.*

Pass the front strand, No. 1 in Figure A of Plate XXXII, to the right under the right strand, No. 2, and then work it under the cross strand which is on top of the right strand, bringing it out at the center of the square. Do not pull the strand all through; leave a loop of it about one-half inch long. (Figure B.) Pass the right strand, No. 2, (about which the first loop was formed) under the back

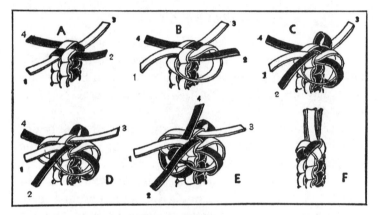

PLATE XXXII

strand, No. 3, then work it under the cross strand which is on top of the back strand, bringing it out at the center of the square. Leave a small loop as you draw the strand through. (Figure C.) Similarly pass the back strand, No. 3, under the left strand, No. 4, then work it under the cross strand which is on top of the left strand, and out at the center of the square, leaving a small loop. (Figure D.) Then bring the left strand, No. 4, to the front and pass it through the loop formed by the first strand, work it under the cross strand which is on top of the first strand and bring it out at the center of the square, leaving a small loop. (Figure E.) Take the four ends, which are now all at the center of the square, and draw them up evenly until all the little loops have disappeared. (Figure F.) Then pull the work together very tight.

(2). *When front strand is on right half of front.*

If the front strand is on the right half of the front, the process is the same as already described except that the work must be done to the left instead of to the right. Pass the front strand, No. 1, to the left under the left strand, No. 4, and then work it under the cross strand which is on top of the left strand, bringing it out at the center of the square. Do not pull the strand all through; leave a loop of it about one-half inch long. Pass the left strand, No. 4 (about which the first loop was formed), under the back strand, No. 3, then work it under the cross strand which is on top of the back strand and out at the center of the square, leaving a small loop as you draw the strand through. Similarly pass the back strand, No. 3, under the right strand, No. 2, then work it under the cross strand which is on top of the right strand and out at the center of the square, leaving a small loop. Then pass the right strand, No. 2, through the loop formed by the first strand, work it under the cross strand which is on top of the first strand and out at the center of the square, leaving a small loop. Take the four ends, which are now all at the center of the square, and draw them up evenly until all the little loops have disappeared. Then pull the work together very tight.

After the lock knot is made, either cut the strands off close to the work or clip them off about an inch from the knot and point the ends. The knot and the little ends give the effect of a tassel.

CHAPTER VI

ARTICLES OF SOLID BRAIDING

THE articles of solid braiding described in this chapter are all made of coated gimp, because of its attractiveness and its special suitability for these braiding processes. This gimp consists of tape coated with pyroxylin, which gives it a glossy finish resembling patent leather in many beautiful colors. It is very strong and durable and can be washed off with water. The gimp is made either flat or round. The flat gimp has the edges folded in so that an almost imperceptible join extends down the middle of the wrong side. It is obtainable in two widths, one-eighth inch and one-fourth inch. Round gimp is also made in two sizes, the smaller being like fine cord. Gimp is inexpensive, about two cents a yard; a quality called "de luxe," with silver or gilt edges, is slightly higher.

Articles of solid braiding may be made with all the strands of the same color, but combinations of two harmonizing colors are usually preferable. Some effective combinations are: any color combined with white or black; light brown with dark brown; medium brown with orange; red, green or blue with silver or gold.

Braided Bracelet on Metal Band

MATERIALS:

    Band of thin metal, ¾ in. wide

    4 lengths of coated gimp, each length 2¼ yds. long

The length of the metal band required for the bracelet shown in Plate XXXIII depends on the size desired for the bracelet. For a large hand, the band should be 10 inches long; for a medium-sized hand, 9½ inches; for a child's hand, 9 inches. The metal can be cut with metal shears.

PLATE XXXIII

After the band has been cut to the size desired, ½ inch from one end, make a straight cut to a depth of a little more than half across the band. Then make the cut into a very narrow V-shape by clipping off each side at a slight diagonal. Make a similar cut ½ inch from the other end of the band, but on the opposite side from the first cut, as shown in Figure A of Plate XXXIV. Insert one cut through the other to form the bracelet as shown in Figure B. Put the bracelet on any solid surface and pound with a mallet until the edges fit smoothly together.

The gimp is to be braided around the band by the same method as was described on page 66 for starting the braiding of two lengths over a strip of cardboard.

Find the centers of the four lengths of gimp and arrange the lengths in whatever order you wish. The simplest arrangements are as follows: (1) two lengths of one color and two lengths of another, arranged so that the colors alternate, will give the diagonal effect shown in the first bracelet; (2) two lengths of one color followed by two lengths of the other will give alternating diamond-shaped blocks as in the second bracelet; (3) three lengths of one color followed by one length of the other will give broader diamond blocks of the predominating color. Other effects can be obtained by looping the strands at the back as shown on Plate XXVI.

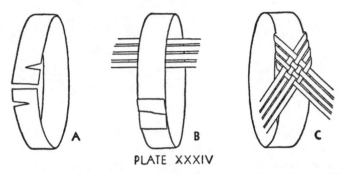

PLATE XXXIV

Hold the four lengths at their centers across the inside of the bracelet as shown in Figure B of Plate XXXIV. The wrong sides of the gimp should be against the inside of the bracelet. Start the work an inch or more from the join in the metal, which will be easily and imperceptibly covered in the course of the braiding. While you hold the work firmly between your left thumb and forefinger, weave the four right strands through the four left strands on the front of the bracelet, as shown in Figure C. Make sure that all the strands are right-side up on the front of the bracelet and that none have been twisted on the inside. Pull the work up tight so that the interwoven strands will lie flat against the metal band with no feeling of bulging.

The braiding from this point is the same as eight-strand round braiding described on page 64. Start with the upper right strand. Pass this strand through the bracelet, guiding it with your right forefinger to keep it from twisting, bring it out at the left between the third and second strands from the bottom, then bring it over the second strand and under the first strand, back to the right. Then pass the upper left strand through the bracelet, guiding it with your left forefinger, bring it out between the second and third strands at the right, over the second, under the first and back to the left.

Continue in the same way, working with the upper strand first of the right side and then of the left side. If you have to leave your work or at any time become confused as to which strand to use for your next step, examine the last crossing of the strands; if the top strand in the crossing goes to the left, the next strand to use must be the upper right, and vice versa.

When you have worked around the bracelet and have come back to the starting point, you must make your pattern complete. You may have to push your work back closer to allow room to complete the pattern, or, if you have been braiding very tightly so that you cannot push it back, you may have to loosen it a little and pull out the work until the pattern comes together.

When the pattern is complete, you should have four strands on each side in the same order as they were at the start. Of those on the right, the first, second, and third strands will be found to come out to the edge of the bracelet. Of those on the left, the first and second strands will come out to the edge.

Clip off the ends of the strands diagonally to make them pointed. With an awl or any blunt-pointed instrument loosen up the first three strands of the braiding that you made at the beginning and separate them a little so that you can be sure they are in their correct positions.

Work the fourth strand of the right side under the beginning strand on the same side, so that it comes out at the right edge. Then pass the third strand of the left side over one and work it under one and out to the left edge. Pass the fourth strand of the left side over one and work it under one and out to the left edge. All four strands on both sides are now out to their respective edges.

To finish off, the work is done inside the bracelet. Turn the bracelet so that the end of your work is opposite you on the inside of the back. With a blunt-pointed tool loosen the first two diagonal strands made on the inside at the beginning of your work. Pay no attention to the straight strands, as you work right over them.

Turn the first strand on the left inside the bracelet and work it up under the two diagonal strands on the right and out to the edge, but do not pull it tight. Then work the first strand at the right under the strand you have just made and the one next above it and out to the edge. Continue thus first with the strands of the left side and then those of the right, working each under two diagonal strands and out to the edge. When all the strands have been worked in, draw the work up tight and cut the strands off close to the edges of the bracelet.

Boy Scout's Lanyard

MATERIALS:
> 2 lengths of coated gimp in contrasting colors, each
>   3½ yds. long
> Spring clip

The lanyard shown in Plate XXXV is made so that one end of the loop will slide on the other, thus making it possible to shorten the loop after it has been put over the boy's head.

Pass the two lengths of gimp through the ring of the clip and draw them through until the clip is at the center of the lengths. The two lengths thus form four equal strands. Arrange the strands for four-strand round braid-

PLATE XXXV

ing, as directed on page 66, inserting the little strip of cardboard temporarily, if you need to do so in order to get the strands in the correct position. Be sure that the strands are all right side up in the little diamond that you form to start the braiding. Secure the clip to a vise or other steady object. Remove the cardboard and continue with round braiding until you are within 12 inches of the ends of the strands. Your braided length should be about 39 or 40 inches long.

Remove the work from the article to which it is tied.

Form a long loop by holding the end of the braid against any point in the other length of it. The remaining 12 inches of the four strands are to be used to secure the loop by being braided around the other length of the lanyard as a core. Hold the work between your left thumb and forefinger, with the loop downward. If you are using two colors, arrange the four twelve-inch ends so that the front and back strands are of one color and the right and left strands, of the other color. With the work in this position, make one row of spiral braiding right around the braided core and pull it up firm but not too tight. Then change to square braiding, working around the braided core, and continue the square braiding for about an inch. If you prefer, you may continue with spiral braiding for this inch, instead of changing to square braiding. This inch of either square or spiral braiding must hold the loop securely, but it should not be so tight that the braided core cannot be pulled through it.

Finish the braiding with a lock knot. Then either cut the ends off close at the center of the knot or leave about an inch of the strands and point them off to give the effect of a little tassel.

Dog Leash

MATERIALS:

> 4 lengths of coated gimp, each 3½ yds. long—preferably in two contrasting colors
> (additional 2 lengths, one of each color, each length 3 yds. long, if the center of the handle is to be reënforced, as in the leash illustrated in Plate XXXVI)
> 1 strong rope core about ⅛ in. thick, 1¾ yds. long
> 1 strong swivel clasp
> 2 short pieces of picture wire

Find the center of the core, 31½ inches from either end, and the centers of the four lengths of gimp, 63 inches from the ends. Lay the lengths of gimp along the core with the centers at the center of the core and tie a string securely, at that point, around the gimp and core.

Measure 15 inches from one end of the core and turn

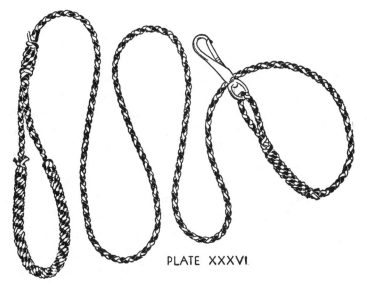

PLATE XXXVI

that end back to the 15 inch point to form the loop for the handle. Hold the end firmly against the other side of the loop, while you wind a piece of picture wire very tightly around both, for about an inch. If the core is made of twisted strands, unravel the end, before you wind the wire on, in order that the join may be less bulky.

Attach the work to a vise or other steady object by means of the string with which you have tied the strands and the core at their centers. Have the end of the core with the handle loop toward you. You are to start braiding where the gimp is tied to the core. Arrange the strands for four-strand round braiding, inserting the strip of cardboard over the core until you have woven your strands into the little diamond, as directed on page 66. Then remove the cardboard and continue with round braiding, passing the working strands from the upper left or right, as the case may be, behind the core and up on the opposite side. Pull the work tight each time after you have brought the working strand back to its original side.

When you come to the join of the loop, continue your round braiding over the join, then down either side, around the loop, and back to within about one-half inch of the join. For the next two or three rows of work, carry the round braiding around both sides of the loop, both the side you are completing and the other side also. Then hold the loop downward between your left thumb and forefinger, and change from round braiding to spiral braiding, making a spiral braid of at least one inch in order to re-enforce the join as strongly as possible. End with a lock knot. Either cut off the strands close to the knot or leave little ends about ¾ inch long, and point them off like a little tassel.

Measure off 5 inches from the other end of the core. Put the swivel clasp on this end and then turn the end up to the 5 inch point and, with the other short piece of picture wire, join it to the other side of the loop in the same way as has been directed for joining the two sides of the handle loop.

Remove the string which you used to tie the gimp strands and the core at their centers and tie it around the finished braiding a few inches back from the start and attach the work to a steady object. Have the unfinished end of the core toward you. The braiding of this half is to be done in the same way as the first half, the small loop is to be braided according to the directions which were given for the larger loop, and the braiding is to be finished off similarly with a lock knot.

If you wish to re-enforce the handle, find the center of the top of the handle loop and measure down on either side about 4 inches. With a steel knitting needle or other blunt-pointed instrument, work an opening under a couple of strands of the braid from back to front at this point and pass one of the 3 yard lengths of gimp, wrongside up, through the opening. Pull the gimp half through so that you have strands of equal length at the back and front. Similarly work another opening at the same point from left to right and work the other length through, wrong-side up. With these four strands, make spiral braiding over the round-braid as a core until you reach a point on the opposite side of the loop at the same distance, 4 inches, from the top. Finish with a lock knot and cut the ends close or clip them off to form a tassel.

PART II KNOTTING

CHAPTER VII

Different Kinds of Knots

Origin of Knotting

THE knotting of cords together for ornamental or practical uses is of very ancient origin. The art was especially developed by the Arabians, particularly for making elaborate fringes, called "macramé." This word has since been loosely used to refer to the knotting processes, without regard for its proper restricted meaning.

There are comparatively few fundamental knots, but they can be developed and combined with almost limitless variation into more or less intricate patterns. These processes were the basis of the fine pillow laces, which were originated in Genoa, Italy, in the sixteenth century and have since been extended to other European countries and even to South America. Knotting of heavier strands, which was continued mostly in convents during the Middle Ages, has been extensively practiced by seamen, who have often produced articles with great ingenuity and dexterity. The seamen have, in many instances, adopted special names for the knots, so that some knots are now known by two different names. In fact, some knots which are used mostly in fine work are called stitches, instead of knots.

Cords for Knotting

Any kind of strong thread or cord—silk, rayon, cotton, or linen—may be used for knotting, but it must either be woven or have a strong twist so that it will not stretch or fray in the handling during the process of the work. It is not practical to attempt to make knotted articles with loosely twisted threads or cords or with those of a springy type which cannot be tied tight. The knots of the illustrations were made with cords and the word "cord" will be used in describing them, though the worker may prefer to use some kind of strong thread.

Square or Flat Knots

The most useful kind of knot is called either the "square" or "flat" knot. It is made by knotting two strands, No. 1 and No. 2 in Figure A of Plate XXXVII,

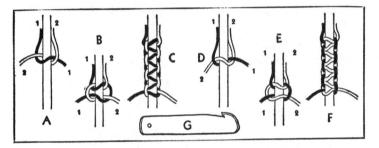

PLATE XXXVII

over a central core. The core may be of the same cord as the working strands or it may be of any other kind of cord or of any other suitable material. The working strands must be three and a half or more times the length of the core. The finer the cord is which is used for the working strands, the longer the strands must be in proportion to the core.

The top ends of the strands and the core must be fastened securely to some steady object.

The core must always be kept taut, while you are

making a square knot over it. A simple way of holding the core is to wind the lower end around the
shank of a button, if you are wearing a coat, sweater, or
other garment with a button at your waist. Some work-
ers, especially seamen, use a hook for securing the core,
similar to that shown in Figure G. It may be sawed out
of a narrow piece of wood, cut from heavy cardboard,
or filed from the handle of a discarded toothbrush. A
string is passed through the hole in the hook and tied
around the worker's waist. The core is secured by twisting it around the hook or the button; it will hold without
being tied. During the work, the core should be kept just
taut, but not pulled.

To make a square knot, start with the left strand, No.
1 in Figure A. Leaving a small loop of the strand at the
left, pass the strand over the core and leave it in horizontal position at the right. Then bring the right strand,
No. 2, over No. 1 at the right, pass it behind the core, and
out at the left through the loop of No. 1 which was left
at the start. This completes the first step. For the second
step, bring No. 1 back to the left over the core, leaving
a small loop of No. 1 at the right. Then bring No. 2 at
the left over No. 1, pass it behind the core, and bring it
out at the right through the loop of No. 1, as shown in
Figure B. These two steps make the knot. Continue in
the same way, giving the effect shown in Figure C. This
is called a right-handed square knot.

The process may be reversed, first bringing the right
strand, No. 2, over the core, after leaving a small loop of
No. 2 at the right, and then passing No. 1 over No. 2,
behind the core, and out at the right through the loop of
No. 2 for the first step. (Figure D.) For the second step
bring No. 2 back to the right over the core, leaving a

small loop at the left, and then bring No. 1 over No. 2, behind the core and out at the left through the loop of No. 2. (Figure E.) This is called a left-handed knot. If the strands are of different colors, the effect of a left-handed knot will be different from that of a right-handed knot, as shown in Figure F.

Spiral Square Knotting

A right spiral effect, shown in Figure A of Plate XXXVIII, is obtained by using only the first step of a right-handed knot repeatedly, without using the second step. A left spiral effect, shown in Figure B, is obtained by

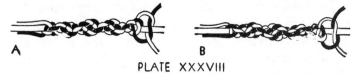

PLATE XXXVIII

using only the first step of a left-handed knot repeatedly, without using the second step. It usually requires six half knots to make one complete twist and it is best to make all six half knots loosely over the core and then pull them tight, one at a time. To reverse a spiral, make the spiral either to the left or to the right for as long as you wish, then make one complete square knot, and continue with the spiral in the other direction.

Square Knotting over Cores of the Same Cord

The core of a square knot, as has been previously stated, may be of any suitable material but, if an article such as a belt, bag, or anything of more than one length of knotting is to be made, the cores consist of **two** strands of the knotting cord. Each length of the cord must be looped over the end or inner bar of a belt buckle or any other horizontal bar or it may be worked through the edge of cloth, if the knotting is to be used for fringe. The bar must be secured very firmly to a steady object. A piece of twine tied across the back of a chair makes **a** satisfactory bar for use in practicing the process.

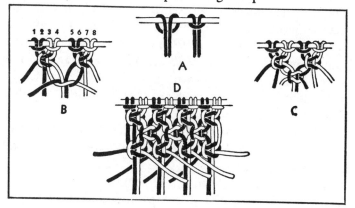

PLATE XXXIX

Find the center of the length of cord and pass it to the back over the bar so that it makes a loop at the back, as shown in Figure A of Plate XXXIX. Then draw the two ends of the cord through this loop and pull them tight. Loop a second length of cord over the bar in the same way. You now have four strands, of which the center two will be the core and the outer left and right will be the working strands. Figure B shows four lengths of cord looped over the bar, making eight strands, or two groups of four strands. In the first row of work, **a** square knot is made with each of these groups. In the first group, strands No. 2 and No. 3 are used as the core, while the knot is made over them with strands No. 1 and 4; in the second group, strands Nos. 6 and 7 are used as the core, while the knot is made over them with strands Nos. 5 and 8. Always secure the core strands to a hook or button at your waist and hold them taut, while you make the knot over them.

For the next row of work, the two outer strands at the left and similarly the two outer strands at the right are not used. Of the other four strands, the two middle strands, Nos. 4 and 5, are used as a core, while a square knot is made over them with strands Nos. 3 and 6. The start of this knot is shown in Figure B. In Figure C, the two groups of strands have been moved close together and the knot completed.

For the third row repeat the process of the first row, making two knots. For the fourth row repeat the process of the second row.

Any desired even number of lengths of cord can be looped on the bar, giving groups of strands in multiples of four, to make an article as wide as you wish, as shown in Figure D. Knots of each group of four strands are made for the first row. In the second row, the two outer strands at the left are unused and center knots made with (1) the two right strands of the first knot and the two left strands of the second knot; (2) the two right strands of the second knot and the two left strands of the third knot, and so on across the row. The two outer right strands will also be unused in the second row of work. For the third row, repeat the first row, and continue by alternating the rows in the same way.

Usually each row of knotting is made over the core strands as close as possible to the preceding row, as in the sample illustrated in Plate XLII, but an open-work effect may be obtained by making the knots at a distance of an eighth of an inch or more down on the core, as in the bag in Plate LVII.

Right-handed knots are regularly used, but left-handed knots may be substituted at any time, when the color effect of a left-handed knot is desired.

Triple Knot

The Triple Knot, also called a "Double Solomon's Knot," shown in Figure A of Plate XL, consists of the two steps of a regular square knot, followed by the first step

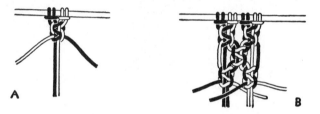

PLATE XL

used again. It is, therefore, really a knot and a half. It may be made either of right-handed or left-handed square knotting. In Figure B, eight strands are used in two groups of four to make two triple knots. In the second row, the two right strands of the first knot and the two left strands of the second knot are used for a center triple knot. In the third row, the processes of the first row are repeated.

Half-Hitch Knot

A Half-Hitch is made by looping a strand of knotting cord once over a core. A single half-hitch will not hold and a second half-hitch is needed to secure it. A half-hitch knot, therefore, consists of two half-hitches. The core may be of the same cord as the knotting strand or it may be of a different cord. The core may be in vertical, horizontal, or diagonal position.

If the core is in vertical position, the knotting strand may be at its left or at its right, as in Figure A of Plate XLI. Pass the knotting strand over the core with a back-

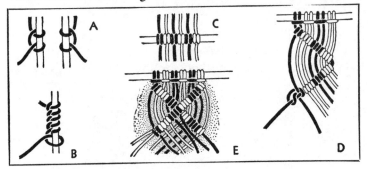

PLATE XLI

ward loop, bringing it under the core and out at the left (or right), over itself. This is the first half-hitch. Then loop the strand again over the core in the same way and bring the end of the strand out over itself. This is the second half-hitch. Pull the knotting strand very tight after the second half-hitch, thus making a half-hitch knot. The term "half-hitching" means making a complete half-hitch knot. A vertical strip of half-hitching is made by repeating the half-hitch knots over the core, which is kept vertical, as in Figure B.

A half-hitch may also be made by passing the working strand first under the core and then over it, as shown in the untightened knot in Figure D.

Frequently the core is laid either horizontally or diagonally on top of a number of strands and each strand in succession is half-hitched over it. In making such horizontal or diagonal bands of half-hitching, the first half-hitch fixes the location of the knot and the direction of the band; the second half-hitch tightens the knot. In these positions the core strand must be held in position with one hand, while the knotting is done with the other hand. It requires practice to get the direction of the band as you wish it and to make the knots uniform. In Figure C, the core is laid horizontally over six knotting strands, each of which is half-hitched over the core.

Often one of the cords of the work is used as a core. In Figure D, the outer left strand was laid diagonally

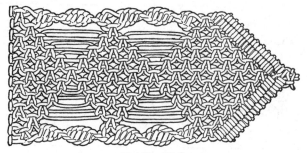

PLATE XLII

across the others and each of the other strands in succession was half-hitched over it. The same strand was then laid diagonally from right to left and half-hitches were made over it again with the other strands. In Figure E, the outer left strand was laid diagonally across the others and half-hitches were made to the center. The outer right strand was then laid diagonally to the left and half-hitches were made with all the other strands. The half-hitching over the left core strand was then completed to

the right. The pattern formed by two meeting or crossing bands of diagonal half-hitching is sometimes called a
"galoon."

Diagonal bands of half-hitching are frequently used to
end off square knotted work in belts and other articles.
Plate XLII shows a section of square knotting, with
spiral square knotting at the sides, the square knotting
then brought to a point and finished with diagonal bars
of half-hitching.

Picot Tops

The use of horizontal bars of half-hitching makes it
possible to form picot tops for square knotting, which
are especially attractive as headings for fringes.

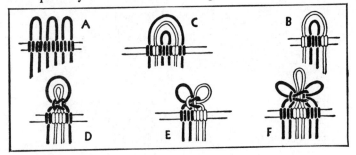

PLATE XLIII

To hold the loops of the cord in place you must use a
steady, firm, well-stuffed cushion with strong pins set
in the cushion in whatever arrangement you wish. A
brick, wrapped around with a roll of cotton wadding and
then covered with unbleached cotton fastened on firmly,
makes a satisfactory substitute for a cushion. The pins
should have large enough heads so that the cords will not
slip off when the knots are being tied. Large glass-headed
pins are the most satisfactory.

The picot tops may be very simple or they may be made as intricate as you wish. Figure A of Plate XLIII shows the simplest type. Loop each length of cord around a pin, forming two strands. Lay a core of the same kind of cord or any other cord on top of the strands horizontally below the picots and half-hitch each strand over this core. Figure B shows an arrangement of a double picot and Figure C, of a triple picot. For the effect shown in Figure D, arrange the cords first as in Figure B. Then use the two outer strands to make a square knot over the two middle strands, and half-hitch all the strands over a horizontal core. For Figure E, arrange the two loops first as in Figure A. Then use the outer strands of the two picots to make a square knot over the center strands and half-hitch all the strands over a horizontal core.

Three loops, with the middle one higher than the others, are grouped together in Figure F. Use the outer strands of the first and third loops to make a large collecting knot over the other strands, described on the next page. Then half-hitch all the strands over a horizontal core.

Collecting Knots

Small Collecting Knot. A small collecting knot is used to connect three or more strands. In Figure A of Plate XLIV, the outer right strand is thus used to connect this strand with the two strands at its left. Make a loop to the right with the strand to be used, bringing the strand over itself toward the other strands. Hold the loop with your thumb and forefinger while you pass the end of the strand over the other strands and then behind them and out through the loop. Pull the strand tight so that the knot is brought behind the strands and only the crossing shows in front, as in Figure B. If you wish to use the left strand for the collecting knot, you must make the loop to the left, then bring the end of the strand over the other strands and continue as in the directions for the use of the right strand.

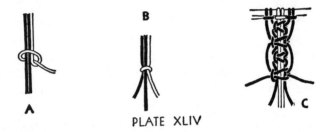

PLATE XLIV

Large Collecting Knot. A large collecting knot is a square knot made over a core of more than two strands. In Figure C, three lengths of cord are knotted onto a bar, forming six strands. Strands Nos. 2 and 5 are first used to form a square knot, over Nos. 3 and 4 as a core, while Nos. 1 and 6 are unused. Then strands Nos. 1 and 6 are used to form a large collecting knot, which is made in just the same way as a square knot, over strands Nos. 2, 3, 4, and 5 together. A second square knot is made with the four inner strands and then a second large collecting knot with strands Nos. 1 and 6 over the inner strands. The square knots have been used in the illustration before the large collecting knots to show their similarity, but they are not needed in making a large collecting knot, which may be made over any group of more than two strands.

Chain Stitch

The Single Chain Stitch, shown in Figures A and B of Plate XLV, is made with two lengths of cord, each of which is used alternately as a core and as a working strand. Loop the right strand over the left strand (or vice versa) in the same way as in making a single half-hitch stitch. Then loop the left strand over the right strand (or vice versa). Continue by making a loop alter-

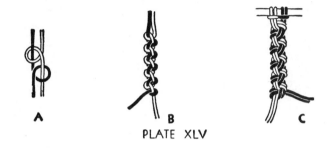

PLATE XLV

nately with the right strand over the left, followed by a loop with the left strand over the right.

A double chain stitch, shown in Figure C, is made with two double strands, each pair of strands being looped alternately over the other pair in the same way as described for a single chain stitch.

Buttonhole Stitches

A Single Buttonhole Stitch, shown in Figure A of Plate XLVI, is made with two lengths of the same or different cords, one of which is used as a core, the other, as a working strand. Loop the working strand over the core in the same way as in making a single half-hitch stitch. A single buttonhole stitch is, in fact, identical with a half-hitch, but it is treated separately here as a basis for the other stitches which follow.

A Double Buttonhole Stitch shown in Figure B, consists of two loops of a working strand over a core strand. Make the first loop over the core in the same way as in making a single buttonhole stitch or a single half-hitch stitch. In making the second loop, pass the working strand under the core, then bring it over the core and down behind itself.

A Waved Buttonhole, shown in Figure C, consists of a

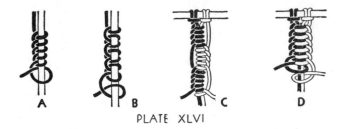

PLATE XLVI

series of single buttonhole stitches made with the outer left strand over a core, followed by a similar series made with the outer right strand over the same core. In the illustration, the core consists of two strands of the same knotting cord as the outer working strands, but the waved buttonhole may be similarly made over any core.

The Basket Stitch, shown in Figure D, consists of a single buttonhole stitch made over a core with an outer working strand on one side, followed by a single buttonhole stitch made over the same core with the outer working strand on the other side. In the illustration the core consists of two strands of the same cord as the working strands, but any kind of core may be used.

Sennit Stitch

The Sennit Stitch, shown in Figure A of Plate XLVII, is really braiding, not knotting. It is done in the same way as four-strand round braiding, the directions for which have been given on page 60.

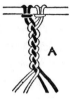 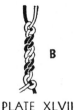 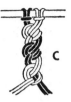

PLATE XLVII

Bullion Stitch

The Bullion Stitch, shown in Figure B of Plate XLVII, is made with two strands of knotting cord. Attach the strands to a steady object. Hold the left strand slanting diagonally to the right as a core, while you loop the right strand over and under it twice, in the same way as directed for buttonhole stitches on page 103. This completes one bullion stitch. The end of the knotting strand will be at the left after the second loop has been made with it. In the next stitch, this strand is used as a core, while the knotting is done with the other strand. Therefore, hold the new core strand slanting diagonally to the right, while you make a bullion stitch over it with the other strand. Continue by using the two strands alternately, first as the core strand and then as the knotting strand. The bullion stitch slants to the right by this method. To make it slant toward the left, instead of toward the right, hold the right strand slanting diagonally to the left as a core and make the bullion stitch over it with the left strand. Continue in the same way, each time using the strand which is at the right as a core and the strand which is at the left as the knotting strand.

A Double Bullion Stitch, made with two double strands, is shown in Figure C. It illustrates the process more clearly than the single stitch.

Triangle Stitch

The Triangle Stitch, shown in Figure A of Plate XLVIII, is made with two strands of knotting cord. Make an open loop to the right with the left strand, without crossing the strand over itself. Hold the loop between your left thumb and forefinger. Bring the right strand down over the loop and up behind it, so that it comes out at the left of itself. Then cross it over itself and down through the loop at its curved end. Let the loop go and

PLATE XLVIII

pull up both strands to tighten the knot. The directions for the use of the two strands may be reversed, if desired.

The first row of Figure B shows four triangle stitches made with four pairs of strands. In the second row, the outer left and the outer right strands are unused, while triangle stitches are formed with strands Nos., 2 and 3; Nos. 4 and 5, and Nos. 6 and 7. In the third row, the four original groups of two strands each are used for four triangle stitches and the work is continued by repeating these rows alternately.

Square Stitch

The Square Stitch, shown in Figure A of Plate XLIX, is made in a manner somewhat similar to the directions for the triangle stitch. Make an open loop to the right with the left strand without crossing it over itself and then make another loop to the left with it below the first loop. Leave the strand hanging at the right of the second loop and hold these two loops with your thumb and forefinger. Bring the right strand down behind the upper part of the top loop near its curved end and out in front through the top loop. Then bring the strand down over the lower loop, up behind both the lower and upper loops,

A   B

PLATE XLIX

over the top of the upper loop at its open end, then straight down in front, and pass it from front to back through the lower loop. The strands have thus changed places; the original left strand has been brought to the right and the right strand, to the left. Let the loops go and pull both strands to tighten the knot. The directions for the use of the two strands may be reversed, if desired.

The first row of Figure B shows four square stitches made with four pairs of strands. In the second row, the outer left and the outer right strands are unused, while square stitches are made with strands Nos. 2 and 3, Nos. 4 and 5, and Nos. 6 and 7. In the third row, all eight strands are again used for four square stitches, but it will be observed that the strands are not in their original positions. The work is continued by repeating these **rows** alternately.

Shell Knot

A Small Shell Knot, shown in Figure D of Plate L, may be added as a decorative unit in any work where four strands are used. The two center strands are used as a core, while the outer strands are used for the knotting. To form the shell knot, first make three or four square knots over the core with the knotting strands, as in Figure A. Then insert the ends of the core strands

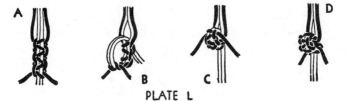

PLATE L

through the work above the first square knot (Figure B), and pull them down at the back until the end of the last square knot has been brought up tight with the work (Figure C). Then, using the same knotting strands which were used for the series of square knots, make a square knot over the core strands under the shell. This square knot is needed to hold the shell and completes the shell knot. (Figure D.)

If both knotting strands are of the same color, it is advisable to bring the left one to the right and the right one to the left at the top of the shell before you make the square knot under the shell. This step will serve to hold the top of the shell tighter, but it is not absolutely necessary and will reverse the knotting strands, which may not be desirable when they are of different colors.

A large shell knot may be made when eight strands are available. The process is the same as for the small shell. Use the middle four strands as a core and work with double knotting strands.

Chinese Knot

There are several Chinese and Japanese knots, but most of them are complicated and require such lengthy directions that they cannot be included in this manual. The Chinese knot shown in Plate LI has been selected for

PLATE LI

description because of its comparative simplicity. It is made with a single length of cord.

Lay the cord on a flat surface with the center of the strand at the top, and cross the left end over the right end so as to form a loop of whatever size you wish. This will be the central loop of the knot, and crossing will be at the middle of the bottom of the knot. The left end of the cord has been transferred to the right by the crossing. Bring this end up on the right and, leaving a loop at the right, simply lay the strand from right to left across both sides of the central loop and leave it in horizontal position at the left. Then, taking the original right end of the cord, which was transferred to the left by the crossing which formed the central loop, bring it up at the left, over the end of the other strand and, leaving a loop at the left, pass it under the left side of the central loop, over the other strand in the middle of the loop, under the right side of the loop so that it comes out in the right loop, and then bring it down over the bottom of the right loop. Pull both strands to make the loops even. The loops at the right and left should be of the same size; the central loop may be of the same size as the side loops or it may be larger or smaller, as desired.

A Chinese knot made with two lengths of cord, used together as a double strand, is shown in Figure B; a knot with triple strands, in Figure C.

Double Carrick Bend

A Double Carrick Bend may be applied as a decorative motif on a flat surface or it may be used as a loop to hold the flap of a hand bag or similar article. It is made of two

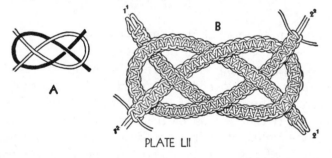

PLATE LII

separate lengths of cord, as shown in Figure A of Plate LII.

Lay one of the strands on a flat surface and form a loop horizontally with it by crossing one end over the other, as shown in the dark loop of Figure A. Place the center of the second strand between the two crossed ends of the first strand. Bring one end of the second strand over the end of the first strand which lies over the other and carry it diagonally under both sides of the loop. Then bring the other end of the second strand under the other end of the first strand, over the nearer side of the loop, under the strand in the middle of the loop, and out over the other side of the loop. Pull the ends of the strands to make the loops even.

Frequently the strands used for a double Carrick bend are doubled or tripled or they may consist of strips of square knotting, as in Figure B. For each strip of square knotting, use two lengths of cord. Insert the first two lengths in your work at the point desired, as at 1^1 of Figure B, so that each length becomes two strands. Use the two inner strands for a core and the two outer strands for working strands and make the strip of square knotting as long as desired. Then insert the other two lengths of cord at a point diagonally opposite the point where the first two lengths were inserted, as at 2^1, and make another strip of knotting of the same length as the first. Form the two strips into a double Carrick bend. Then insert the other ends, 1^2 and 2^2 through the work and secure them by one or two square knots at the back.

Turk's Head

The Turk's Head knot, shown in Plate LIII, is a continuous knot which will encircle the article about which it is formed. It may be made around the top of a tassel, as a loop around a belt or other article, or for any similar use. For practicing the knot, it is best to use a heavy cord or twine and a rather large cylindrical base, such as the handle of a broom or a cardboard mailing tube. Measure around the cylindrical surface and cut one length of cord equal to about eight times this measure.

With your left thumb, hold one end of the cord at any point on the surface of the cylinder (No. 1 of Figure A), while you work entirely with the other end, which will be called the working strand. Wind the work-

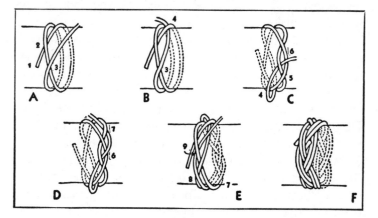

PLATE LIII

ing strand once around the cylinder, then bring it across the first end above where you are holding it with your thumb (No. 2), then again around the cylinder and cross it over itself in front (No. 3), below where it crossed the first end at No. 2. You will observe that you have formed two parallel strands around the back of the cylinder, shown by the dotted lines in Figure A. Pass the working strand from right to left under the right one of the parallel strands above the first crossing, pulling it out between the two parallel strands, and bring it over the left strand. (No. 4 in Figure B.)

Then revolve the cylinder forward toward you so that the last step, at No. 4, is at the bottom of the front.

The next step is to loop the left one of the parallel

strands over the right one above the point where the working strand came out between them (No. 5 in Figure C) and hold the loop with one forefinger. Bring the working strand from the left under the left side of this loop, out in the center of the loop, and cross it over the right side of the loop. (No. 6 in Figure C.)

You will find that you have two seemingly parallel strands left above the loop with which you have just been working, though the left one of the strands really crosses the right strand twice at the ends of a long loop. Pass your working strand from right to left under the right one of these strands, and bring it out between the two strands. (No. 7 in Figure D.) Revolve the cylinder forward again so that the last step, at No. 7, is at the bottom. Then cross the working strand over the left strand, No. 8 in Figure E.

You have thus carried the working strand entirely around the cylinder and back to the starting point. Bring the working strand to the right of the short end and, keeping it beside this strand, pass it under the same strand that crosses the other. (No. 9 in Figure E.) From this point on, you simply carry your working strand along beside this strand, bringing it under or over other cross strands, but never crossing the strand it is following, sometimes at its left and sometimes at its right. The working strand will follow the other strand three times around the cylinder and all the strands will be doubled when the working strand is back to the starting point. (Figure F.) If you wish the strands to be tripled, carry the working strand around again. Cut off the ends of the strands or use them to attach the Turk's head to the article on which it is to be used.

CHAPTER VIII

Knotted Articles

THE original use of square knotting was, as has been stated previously, for the making of more or less intricate fringes. As this form of decoration is little used at present, it has not seemed feasible to include the directions or illustration of any special type. A worker, however, who may wish to make a fringe will find that the various knots described in the preceding chapter will enable him to make such combinations as he desires for a simple or elaborate pattern.

The knotting processes are also suitable for and now more generally used for belts, bags, pulls and similar articles. A few simple applications have been selected for illustration and description.

Shade or Electric Light Pull

MATERIAL:

Any firm cord or string of cotton, linen, rayon, or silk. Each pull requires a length of cord about 12 times as long as the length desired for the pull. A tassel requires about 23 feet.

The shade or electric light pull, shown in Plate LIV, is made by knotting two working strands over a core consisting of four strands of the same cord. Cut two lengths of the cord, twice as long as you wish the pull to be. Attach both lengths to a steady object, each length making two strands. These four strands are to be the core. Secure the ends of the core strands to a hook or button at your waist.

Cut another length of cord about ten times the length desired for the pull. Place the middle of this length behind the core strands at a point about one and one-half or two inches from the top. This length forms the two working strands, which you use for square knotting over the core. The illustration shows a length

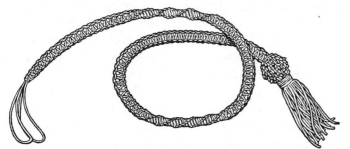

PLATE LIV

of square knotting, followed by a section of spiral, another section of square knotting, another section of spiral, and a final section of square knotting. The entire length may, if preferred, be made of square knotting or various other stitches described in the preceding chapter may be effectively introduced. Do not make knots to the ends of the strands; at least two inches must be left for tying on the tassel.

The directions for starting the pull allow for two lengths (4 strands) of the cord to pass through the hole in the shade stick or the ring to which the pull is to be attached, when finished. If your cord is strong enough, you may prefer to have only one length (2 strands) above the knotted section. In this case, attach only one length to the steady object. Then tie the second length at its center to the two strands formed by the first length at the point where you wish to start the square knotting, making the four-strand core. Begin the square knotting at that point with the long cord and proceed as already directed.

To make the tassel: Cut about twenty-five lengths of cord, twice as long as you wish the tassel to be, and lay them in a lengthwise pile with the ends about even on both sides. Cut ten lengths about two inches longer than the others and lay the ten lengths on top of the pile with the ends projecting about an inch on both sides beyond the shorter lengths. Detach the knotted pull and separate the ends of the six strands of the pull so that there are three on each side. Place the pull at the middle of the top of the pile of tassel strands and attach these strands to the pull by tying the three left strands of the pull to the three right strands with a little group of knots. Be careful to keep the ten longer tassel strands on top of the others. With neighboring pairs of these longer strands make little strips of chain stitches for about three-quarters of an inch. There will be five of these little chains on each side of the tassel. Arrange them so that they cover the top of the tassel evenly. Then, holding the top of the tassel with your left thumb and forefinger just at the ends of the little sections of chain stitches, wind a length of cord several times around the tassel. Work the ends into the tassel and sew them securely. Trim off the tassel so that the strands are of uniform length.

Square knotting may be used as a heading for a tassel instead of chain stitching. For square knotting you must have eight or twelve (a multiple of four) longer strands instead of the ten lengths used for the chains. A plain tassel may be made, without either the chain stitches or square knotting, by simply winding a length of cord several times around the tassel at the point desired, as already described. A Turk's head may be worked around the tassel as an effective finish.

Round Gimp Knotted Bracelets

MATERIALS:

    1 piece of ¼ in. flat gimp, twice as long as the size desired for the bracelet

    2 lengths of narrow round gimp in contrasting colors, each length about 40 inches

The bracelets shown in Figure A of Plate LV are made by knotting the strands of narrow gimp over two thicknesses of the flat gimp as a core.

PLATE LV

Roll the strip of flat gimp so that it forms a bracelet of double thickness. Then, using the long strips of narrow round gimp as working strands, start at any point and make square knots over the double thickness of flat gimp as a core. In the lower bracelet shown in Figure A, all the square knots must be either right-handed or left-handed, as preferred. To obtain the effect in the upper bracelet, make four or five right-handed square knots, followed by one left-handed square knot and similarly alternate sections of right-handed knots and single left-handed knots around the bracelet.

When you are nearing the starting point, lay the ends of the beginnings of the working strands with the core and make the knots over them also, so that they will be worked in out of sight. At the end, cut off the working strands, leaving only short ends and, using an awl or similar instrument, work these ends in out of sight.

Buttoned Bracelet

MATERIAL:
> 2 lengths of coated gimp, ⅛ in. wide, each length 2 yds.

The buttoned bracelet, shown in Figure B of Plate LV, is made entirely of coated gimp one-eighth of an inch wide. Cut off about 5 inches of each of the two-yard lengths. Place the ends of the long pieces together and measure about 15 inches from one end. At this point lay the two five-inch pieces with the longer ends of the other lengths, placing each short piece with the strand of the corresponding color. Using the two short pieces and the two long lengths, make a four-strand round braid for about 2 inches, following the directions on page 60. This two-inch round braid is to form the loop. Bring the two ends of the braid together and make one more row of round braiding, carrying the braiding strands around the other end of the braid as a core, in order to secure the loop. When the loop has been formed, the two fifteen-inch sections of the long strands, which were measured off at the start, will be brought inside the long strands. The four short ends of the five-inch pieces will also be brought together. The bracelet is to be made by square knotting the long strands over the fifteen-inch ends as a core. The four short ends of the five-inch pieces must also be included in the core until they have been covered. Cut off these little ends so that they will be of different lengths, thus preventing their all ending at the same place, which would make a sudden and very perceptible difference in the width of the bracelet.

Attach the braided loop to a steady object and secure the ends of the core strands to a hook or button at your waist. Use the long strands as working strands, and make a strip of square knotting of the length desired. Then remove the work from the object to which it was tied.

To make the button: First make a four-strand round braid with the same four strands which you have been using for the knotting. This round braid is for the shank of the button; it should be about one-fourth inch long. Then, holding the work with the braided section downward between your left'thumb and forefinger, make one row of spiral braiding, crossing the strands to the left. Invert the work so that the braided section is upward and make one row of spiral braiding, crossing the strands to the right. Proceed in this way with spiral braiding, making one row on top with the strands carried to the left, followed by one row on the bottom with the strands carried to the right, until the button is of the desired size. Make the last row of spiral braiding on the bottom, follow it by one row of square braiding also on the bottom, and end it off with a lock knot, described on page 75.

Belt

MATERIALS:

> Cotton, linen, rayon, or silk cord in contrasting light
> and dark colors
> Belt buckle

The cord selected for the belt shown in Plate LVI must
be firm and heavy. The belt buckle should have a middle
bar, onto which the cords are to be knotted, equal in
width to twelve strands of cord. A buckle either with or

PLATE LVI

without a pin may be used; the holes made in the center
of the belt at the places where the light color extends
across serve as eyelets for the pin.

Cut two lengths of the dark cord and four lengths of
the light cord, each length seven times the length desired
for the belt. Some of the light strands are used only as
core strands and do not need to be much longer than the
belt length, but, as it would be confusing to one who is
making the belt for the first time to try to differentiate
the strands, it is better to cut them all of the same length
even though some very long ends will have to be cut
off when the belt is completed.

Attach the belt buckle to a steady object, and knot onto
the bar one length of the dark cord, dividing it evenly;
then knot on similarly the four light cords, and lastly the
second dark cord. The six lengths thus make twelve

strands, or three groups of four strands each for square knotting.

While making the knots, always attach the core strands to a button or hook at your belt; also tie with loose loops the groups of strands which are not being used.

In the first group of four strands, the two dark strands are to be knotted over the first pair of light strands as a core. First pass the right dark strand over the light strands so that it is at their right. Then make five square knots with the dark strands over the light ones. The next two pairs of light strands form the second group of four strands, the outer left and right strands being the knotting strands and the two middle strands, the core. Make five square knots. In the third group, the remaining pair of light strands are to be the core and the pair of dark strands are to be the knotting strands. First bring the outer left dark strand across the light core strands and hold a loop of it under your thumb until you have made the first square knot. Make a total of five square knots, as you did with the other two groups.

For the next row of work, the two outer strands, one dark and one light, at the left and a similar pair at the right are to be unused, while two square knots are made with the remaining eight strands. For the first knot, the third and fourth strands of the first group become the core, while the first two strands of the middle group are knotted over them. Bring the left of the middle group of strands over the core strands, holding a loop of it under your thumb until the knot is made. For the second knot, the first and second strands of the third group become the core, while the third and fourth strands of the middle group are knotted over them. Bring the fourth strand of the middle group over the first and second strands of the third group and make one square knot with the third and fourth strands of the middle group.

In the next row return the strands to their previous positions and make a second series of five square knots with each of the three groups. Continue by alternating the strips of five knots in three groups with one row consisting of two inner square knots, until the belt is of the required length. Then bring the work to a point by making a few more knots in the center group than in the side groups. Lay the outer left strand across the next five strands diagonally to the center and half-hitch the five strands over it very firmly. Similarly lay the outer right strand diagonally across to the center and half-hitch the other five strands over it. At the point of the end, use these two core strands of the half-hitching as a core and knot the two neighboring strands over them with two square knots.

To finish the end, you may either cut off the strands just a slight distance from the bars of half-hitching or turn the ends back inside the belt. When the ends are turned back, if the cord is fine enough, you may thread each strand separately onto a large needle and draw it into the work; otherwise, sew the ends down securely on the inside of the belt.

Knotted Bag

MATERIALS:

> 150 yds. silkateen or twisted pure silk of similar thickness—either in a single color or two contrast-ing colors
>
> 1 pair of narrow rings large enough to slip over the wearer's hand

¼ yd. silk or satin for lining of a matching **or con-**trasting color

PLATE LVII

The knotted bag shown in Plate LVII may be made **of** any strings **or** cords suitable for knotting, but, because of its dainty design, silkateen or silk is recommended. If a heavier knotting cord is used, fewer strands will be needed. A bag made according to the following directions will be about 6½ inches wide and 5¼ inches deep, plus fringe of whatever length you wish.

Cut 80 lengths of silkateen or silk, each length being about 60 inches long. Hang one of the rings on the projecting top of a side rail of a chair and loop 40 lengths onto this ring, making 80 strands. Make square knots with each group of 4 strands, using the 2 middle strands for the core and the first and fourth strands for the working strands. You will thus make 20 square knots across. The last three or four knots at the left and at the right will be considerably higher than the others, due to the curve of the ring, and it is advisable to make extra square knots with these groups of four strands to bring the work nearly level across. Therefore, make two extra knots with the first group, one and a half with the second group, one with the third group, and one half with the fourth group, and similarly, in reverse order at the right.

Then, leaving the first and second strands unused, make a row of 19 square knots across. The last two strands will be unused. Then make a row of 20 square knots, using all the strands. Follow it by a second row of 19 square knots. Then, using each set of four strands, make spirals of 11 half knots, which will give two twists. Then make one row of 20 square knots across. If you are using two colors, you may substitute left-handed square knots for the usual right-handed knots at any time when you wish.

Loop the other 40 strands onto the second handle and repeat the directions for the starting which have been given for the work on the first handle.

Return to the work on the first handle and, leaving the first and second strands unused, make 19 square knots across. Then use the last two strands at the right with the first two strands at the left of the strands on the second handle for a square knot. Make 19 square knots across with the strands of this second side. Then use the last two strands of this side with the first two strands of the first side for a square knot. You will have thus brought the two sides of the bag together. If you wish a deeper opening at the sides, the spirals should be made longer. In making succeeding rows of square knots, work all around the bag, using first strands Nos. 1, 2, 3, and 4, etc., and the next time, Nos. 3, 4, 5, and 6, etc. In this and the following rows, begin gradually to widen the spaces between the knots until they are about $\frac{3}{16}$ inch apart. Make about six or eight rows of square knots around the bag. Then use the groups of four strands for spirals similar to the spirals at the top of the bag. Return to the square knots around the bag for the remaining length of the bag, always spacing them about $\frac{3}{16}$ inch apart.

To make the fringe: Secure the bag by strong pins to a firm cushion, with the bottom edges of the front and back of the bag even. Using two strands from the back as a core and two strands from the front as working strands, make 40 square knots across, pulling them very tight. Then grouping the first six strands at the left, bind them together with a small collecting knot made with either the outer left or outer right strand of the group. The next seventeen groups will consist of four strands each, and the last group, of six strands, all to be bound with small collecting knots. Cut the ends of the fringe even.

To line the bag: Lay the bag on a piece of paper, mark it off, and cut a pattern by which you can cut the material for the lining. Sew the lining with finished seams. Insert it in the bag, sew it in along the handle and down the openings of the sides and also secure it at the bottom of the bag.

The processes used in making the knotted bag are also adaptable for making a cover to place over a silk lamp shade, giving a very unusual and beautiful effect. Similarly the directions for the other articles which have been described in this chapter and the directions for other knots in the preceding chapter will suggest to the worker, after a little practice, many different uses for which these easy but interesting processes are suited.

A CATALOG OF SELECTED
DOVER BOOKS
IN ALL FIELDS OF INTEREST

A CATALOG OF SELECTED DOVER
BOOKS IN ALL FIELDS OF INTEREST

CONCERNING THE SPIRITUAL IN ART, Wassily Kandinsky. Pioneering work by father of abstract art. Thoughts on color theory, nature of art. Analysis of earlier masters. 12 illustrations. 80pp. of text. 5⅜ x 8½. 23411-8

ANIMALS: 1,419 Copyright-Free Illustrations of Mammals, Birds, Fish, Insects, etc., Jim Harter (ed.). Clear wood engravings present, in extremely lifelike poses, over 1,000 species of animals. One of the most extensive pictorial sourcebooks of its kind. Captions. Index. 284pp. 9 x 12. 23766-4

CELTIC ART: The Methods of Construction, George Bain. Simple geometric techniques for making Celtic interlacements, spirals, Kells-type initials, animals, humans, etc. Over 500 illustrations. 160pp. 9 x 12. (Available in U.S. only.) 22923-8

AN ATLAS OF ANATOMY FOR ARTISTS, Fritz Schider. Most thorough reference work on art anatomy in the world. Hundreds of illustrations, including selections from works by Vesalius, Leonardo, Goya, Ingres, Michelangelo, others. 593 illustrations. 192pp. 7⅛ x 10¼. 20241-0

CELTIC HAND STROKE-BY-STROKE (Irish Half-Uncial from "The Book of Kells"): An Arthur Baker Calligraphy Manual, Arthur Baker. Complete guide to creating each letter of the alphabet in distinctive Celtic manner. Covers hand position, strokes, pens, inks, paper, more. Illustrated. 48pp. 8¼ x 11. 24336-2

EASY ORIGAMI, John Montroll. Charming collection of 32 projects (hat, cup, pelican, piano, swan, many more) specially designed for the novice origami hobbyist. Clearly illustrated easy-to-follow instructions insure that even beginning papercrafters will achieve successful results. 48pp. 8¼ x 11. 27298-2

THE COMPLETE BOOK OF BIRDHOUSE CONSTRUCTION FOR WOODWORKERS, Scott D. Campbell. Detailed instructions, illustrations, tables. Also data on bird habitat and instinct patterns. Bibliography. 3 tables. 63 illustrations in 15 figures. 48pp. 5¼ x 8½. 24407-5

BLOOMINGDALE'S ILLUSTRATED 1886 CATALOG: Fashions, Dry Goods and Housewares, Bloomingdale Brothers. Famed merchants' extremely rare catalog depicting about 1,700 products: clothing, housewares, firearms, dry goods, jewelry, more. Invaluable for dating, identifying vintage items. Also, copyright-free graphics for artists, designers. Co-published with Henry Ford Museum & Greenfield Village. 160pp. 8¼ x 11. 25780-0

HISTORIC COSTUME IN PICTURES, Braun & Schneider. Over 1,450 costumed figures in clearly detailed engravings–from dawn of civilization to end of 19th century. Captions. Many folk costumes. 256pp. 8⅜ x 11¾. 23150-X

STICKLEY CRAFTSMAN FURNITURE CATALOGS, Gustav Stickley and L. & J. G. Stickley. Beautiful, functional furniture in two authentic catalogs from 1910. 594 illustrations, including 277 photos, show settles, rockers, armchairs, reclining chairs, bookcases, desks, tables. 183pp. 6½ x 9¼. 23838-5

AMERICAN LOCOMOTIVES IN HISTORIC PHOTOGRAPHS: 1858 to 1949, Ron Ziel (ed.). A rare collection of 126 meticulously detailed official photographs, called "builder portraits," of American locomotives that majestically chronicle the rise of steam locomotive power in America. Introduction. Detailed captions. xi+129pp. 9 x 12. 27393-8

AMERICA'S LIGHTHOUSES: An Illustrated History, Francis Ross Holland, Jr. Delightfully written, profusely illustrated fact-filled survey of over 200 American lighthouses since 1716. History, anecdotes, technological advances, more. 240pp. 8 x 10¾. 25576-X

TOWARDS A NEW ARCHITECTURE, Le Corbusier. Pioneering manifesto by founder of "International School." Technical and aesthetic theories, views of industry, economics, relation of form to function, "mass-production split" and much more. Profusely illustrated. 320pp. 6⅛ x 9¼. (Available in U.S. only.) 25023-7

HOW THE OTHER HALF LIVES, Jacob Riis. Famous journalistic record, exposing poverty and degradation of New York slums around 1900, by major social reformer. 100 striking and influential photographs. 233pp. 10 x 7⅞. 22012-5

FRUIT KEY AND TWIG KEY TO TREES AND SHRUBS, William M. Harlow. One of the handiest and most widely used identification aids. Fruit key covers 120 deciduous and evergreen species; twig key 160 deciduous species. Easily used. Over 300 photographs. 126pp. 5⅜ x 8½. 20511-8

COMMON BIRD SONGS, Dr. Donald J. Borror. Songs of 60 most common U.S. birds: robins, sparrows, cardinals, bluejays, finches, more–arranged in order of increasing complexity. Up to 9 variations of songs of each species.

Cassette and manual 99911-4

ORCHIDS AS HOUSE PLANTS, Rebecca Tyson Northen. Grow cattleyas and many other kinds of orchids–in a window, in a case, or under artificial light. 63 illustrations. 148pp. 5⅜ x 8½. 23261-1

MONSTER MAZES, Dave Phillips. Masterful mazes at four levels of difficulty. Avoid deadly perils and evil creatures to find magical treasures. Solutions for all 32 exciting illustrated puzzles. 48pp. 8¼ x 11. 26005-4

MOZART'S DON GIOVANNI (DOVER OPERA LIBRETTO SERIES), Wolfgang Amadeus Mozart. Introduced and translated by Ellen H. Bleiler. Standard Italian libretto, with complete English translation. Convenient and thoroughly portable–an ideal companion for reading along with a recording or the performance itself. Introduction. List of characters. Plot summary. 121pp. 5¼ x 8½. 24944-1

TECHNICAL MANUAL AND DICTIONARY OF CLASSICAL BALLET, Gail Grant. Defines, explains, comments on steps, movements, poses and concepts. 15-page pictorial section. Basic book for student, viewer. 127pp. 5⅜ x 8½. 21843-0

THE CLARINET AND CLARINET PLAYING, David Pino. Lively, comprehensive work features suggestions about technique, musicianship, and musical interpretation, as well as guidelines for teaching, making your own reeds, and preparing for public performance. Includes an intriguing look at clarinet history. "A godsend," *The Clarinet,* Journal of the International Clarinet Society. Appendixes. 7 illus. 320pp. 5⅜ x 8½. 40270-3

HOLLYWOOD GLAMOR PORTRAITS, John Kobal (ed.). 145 photos from 1926-49. Harlow, Gable, Bogart, Bacall; 94 stars in all. Full background on photographers, technical aspects. 160pp. 8⅜ x 11¼. 23352-9

THE ANNOTATED CASEY AT THE BAT: A Collection of Ballads about the Mighty Casey/Third, Revised Edition, Martin Gardner (ed.). Amusing sequels and parodies of one of America's best-loved poems: Casey's Revenge, Why Casey Whiffed, Casey's Sister at the Bat, others. 256pp. 5⅜ x 8½. 28598-7

THE RAVEN AND OTHER FAVORITE POEMS, Edgar Allan Poe. Over 40 of the author's most memorable poems: "The Bells," "Ulalume," "Israfel," "To Helen," "The Conqueror Worm," "Eldorado," "Annabel Lee," many more. Alphabetic lists of titles and first lines. 64pp. 5³⁄₁₆ x 8¼. 26685-0

PERSONAL MEMOIRS OF U. S. GRANT, Ulysses Simpson Grant. Intelligent, deeply moving firsthand account of Civil War campaigns, considered by many the finest military memoirs ever written. Includes letters, historic photographs, maps and more. 528pp. 6⅛ x 9¼. 28587-1

ANCIENT EGYPTIAN MATERIALS AND INDUSTRIES, A. Lucas and J. Harris. Fascinating, comprehensive, thoroughly documented text describes this ancient civilization's vast resources and the processes that incorporated them in daily life, including the use of animal products, building materials, cosmetics, perfumes and incense, fibers, glazed ware, glass and its manufacture, materials used in the mummification process, and much more. 544pp. 6⅛ x 9¼. (Available in U.S. only.) 40446-3

RUSSIAN STORIES/RUSSKIE RASSKAZY: A Dual-Language Book, edited by Gleb Struve. Twelve tales by such masters as Chekhov, Tolstoy, Dostoevsky, Pushkin, others. Excellent word-for-word English translations on facing pages, plus teaching and study aids, Russian/English vocabulary, biographical/critical introductions, more. 416pp. 5⅜ x 8½. 26244-8

PHILADELPHIA THEN AND NOW: 60 Sites Photographed in the Past and Present, Kenneth Finkel and Susan Oyama. Rare photographs of City Hall, Logan Square, Independence Hall, Betsy Ross House, other landmarks juxtaposed with contemporary views. Captures changing face of historic city. Introduction. Captions. 128pp. 8¼ x 11. 25790-8

AIA ARCHITECTURAL GUIDE TO NASSAU AND SUFFOLK COUNTIES, LONG ISLAND, The American Institute of Architects, Long Island Chapter, and the Society for the Preservation of Long Island Antiquities. Comprehensive, well-researched and generously illustrated volume brings to life over three centuries of Long Island's great architectural heritage. More than 240 photographs with authoritative, extensively detailed captions. 176pp. 8¼ x 11. 26946-9

NORTH AMERICAN INDIAN LIFE: Customs and Traditions of 23 Tribes, Elsie Clews Parsons (ed.). 27 fictionalized essays by noted anthropologists examine religion, customs, government, additional facets of life among the Winnebago, Crow, Zuni, Eskimo, other tribes. 480pp. 6⅛ x 9¼. 27377-6

FRANK LLOYD WRIGHT'S DANA HOUSE, Donald Hoffmann. Pictorial essay of residential masterpiece with over 160 interior and exterior photos, plans, elevations, sketches and studies. 128pp. 9¹/₄ x 10¾. 29120-0

THE MALE AND FEMALE FIGURE IN MOTION: 60 Classic Photographic Sequences, Eadweard Muybridge. 60 true-action photographs of men and women walking, running, climbing, bending, turning, etc., reproduced from rare 19th-century masterpiece. vi + 121pp. 9 x 12. 24745-7

1001 QUESTIONS ANSWERED ABOUT THE SEASHORE, N. J. Berrill and Jacquelyn Berrill. Queries answered about dolphins, sea snails, sponges, starfish, fishes, shore birds, many others. Covers appearance, breeding, growth, feeding, much more. 305pp. 5¼ x 8¼. 23366-9

ATTRACTING BIRDS TO YOUR YARD, William J. Weber. Easy-to-follow guide offers advice on how to attract the greatest diversity of birds: birdhouses, feeders, water and waterers, much more. 96pp. 5³/₁₆ x 8¼. 28927-3

MEDICINAL AND OTHER USES OF NORTH AMERICAN PLANTS: A Historical Survey with Special Reference to the Eastern Indian Tribes, Charlotte Erichsen-Brown. Chronological historical citations document 500 years of usage of plants, trees, shrubs native to eastern Canada, northeastern U.S. Also complete identifying information. 343 illustrations. 544pp. 6½ x 9¼. 25951-X

STORYBOOK MAZES, Dave Phillips. 23 stories and mazes on two-page spreads: Wizard of Oz, Treasure Island, Robin Hood, etc. Solutions. 64pp. 8¼ x 11. 23628-5

AMERICAN NEGRO SONGS: 230 Folk Songs and Spirituals, Religious and Secular, John W. Work. This authoritative study traces the African influences of songs sung and played by black Americans at work, in church, and as entertainment. The author discusses the lyric significance of such songs as "Swing Low, Sweet Chariot," "John Henry," and others and offers the words and music for 230 songs. Bibliography. Index of Song Titles. 272pp. 6½ x 9¼. 40271-1

MOVIE-STAR PORTRAITS OF THE FORTIES, John Kobal (ed.). 163 glamor, studio photos of 106 stars of the 1940s: Rita Hayworth, Ava Gardner, Marlon Brando, Clark Gable, many more. 176pp. 8⅜ x 11¼. 23546-7

BENCHLEY LOST AND FOUND, Robert Benchley. Finest humor from early 30s, about pet peeves, child psychologists, post office and others. Mostly unavailable elsewhere. 73 illustrations by Peter Arno and others. 183pp. 5⅜ x 8½. 22410-4

YEKL and THE IMPORTED BRIDEGROOM AND OTHER STORIES OF YIDDISH NEW YORK, Abraham Cahan. Film Hester Street based on *Yekl* (1896). Novel, other stories among first about Jewish immigrants on N.Y.'s East Side. 240pp. 5⅜ x 8½. 22427-9

SELECTED POEMS, Walt Whitman. Generous sampling from *Leaves of Grass*. Twenty-four poems include "I Hear America Singing," "Song of the Open Road," "I Sing the Body Electric," "When Lilacs Last in the Dooryard Bloom'd," "O Captain! My Captain!"—all reprinted from an authoritative edition. Lists of titles and first lines. 128pp. 5³/₁₆ x 8¼. 26878-0

THE BEST TALES OF HOFFMANN, E. T. A. Hoffmann. 10 of Hoffmann's most important stories: "Nutcracker and the King of Mice," "The Golden Flowerpot," etc. 458pp. 5⅜ x 8½. 21793-0

FROM FETISH TO GOD IN ANCIENT EGYPT, E. A. Wallis Budge. Rich detailed survey of Egyptian conception of "God" and gods, magic, cult of animals, Osiris, more. Also, superb English translations of hymns and legends. 240 illustrations. 545pp. 5⅜ x 8½. 25803-3

FRENCH STORIES/CONTES FRANÇAIS: A Dual-Language Book, Wallace Fowlie. Ten stories by French masters, Voltaire to Camus: "Micromegas" by Voltaire; "The Atheist's Mass" by Balzac; "Minuet" by de Maupassant; "The Guest" by Camus, six more. Excellent English translations on facing pages. Also French-English vocabulary list, exercises, more. 352pp. 5⅜ x 8½. 26443-2

CHICAGO AT THE TURN OF THE CENTURY IN PHOTOGRAPHS: 122 Historic Views from the Collections of the Chicago Historical Society, Larry A. Viskochil. Rare large-format prints offer detailed views of City Hall, State Street, the Loop, Hull House, Union Station, many other landmarks, circa 1904-1913. Introduction. Captions. Maps. 144pp. 9⅜ x 12¼. 24656-6

OLD BROOKLYN IN EARLY PHOTOGRAPHS, 1865-1929, William Lee Younger. Luna Park, Gravesend race track, construction of Grand Army Plaza, moving of Hotel Brighton, etc. 157 previously unpublished photographs. 165pp. 8⅞ x 11¾. 23587-4

THE MYTHS OF THE NORTH AMERICAN INDIANS, Lewis Spence. Rich anthology of the myths and legends of the Algonquins, Iroquois, Pawnees and Sioux, prefaced by an extensive historical and ethnological commentary. 36 illustrations. 480pp. 5⅜ x 8½. 25967-6

AN ENCYCLOPEDIA OF BATTLES: Accounts of Over 1,560 Battles from 1479 B.C. to the Present, David Eggenberger. Essential details of every major battle in recorded history from the first battle of Megiddo in 1479 B.C. to Grenada in 1984. List of Battle Maps. New Appendix covering the years 1967-1984. Index. 99 illustrations. 544pp. 6½ x 9¼. 24913-1

SAILING ALONE AROUND THE WORLD, Captain Joshua Slocum. First man to sail around the world, alone, in small boat. One of great feats of seamanship told in delightful manner. 67 illustrations. 294pp. 5⅜ x 8½. 20326-3

ANARCHISM AND OTHER ESSAYS, Emma Goldman. Powerful, penetrating, prophetic essays on direct action, role of minorities, prison reform, puritan hypocrisy, violence, etc. 271pp. 5⅜ x 8½. 22484-8

MYTHS OF THE HINDUS AND BUDDHISTS, Ananda K. Coomaraswamy and Sister Nivedita. Great stories of the epics; deeds of Krishna, Shiva, taken from puranas, Vedas, folk tales; etc. 32 illustrations. 400pp. 5⅜ x 8½. 21759-0

THE TRAUMA OF BIRTH, Otto Rank. Rank's controversial thesis that anxiety neurosis is caused by profound psychological trauma which occurs at birth. 256pp. 5⅜ x 8½. 27974-X

A THEOLOGICO-POLITICAL TREATISE, Benedict Spinoza. Also contains unfinished Political Treatise. Great classic on religious liberty, theory of government on common consent. R. Elwes translation. Total of 421pp. 5⅜ x 8½. 20249-6

MY BONDAGE AND MY FREEDOM, Frederick Douglass. Born a slave, Douglass became outspoken force in antislavery movement. The best of Douglass' autobiographies. Graphic description of slave life. 464pp. 5⅜ x 8½. 22457-0

FOLLOWING THE EQUATOR: A Journey Around the World, Mark Twain. Fascinating humorous account of 1897 voyage to Hawaii, Australia, India, New Zealand, etc. Ironic, bemused reports on peoples, customs, climate, flora and fauna, politics, much more. 197 illustrations. 720pp. 5⅜ x 8½. 26113-1

THE PEOPLE CALLED SHAKERS, Edward D. Andrews. Definitive study of Shakers: origins, beliefs, practices, dances, social organization, furniture and crafts, etc. 33 illustrations. 351pp. 5⅜ x 8½. 21081-2

THE MYTHS OF GREECE AND ROME, H. A. Guerber. A classic of mythology, generously illustrated, long prized for its simple, graphic, accurate retelling of the principal myths of Greece and Rome, and for its commentary on their origins and significance. With 64 illustrations by Michelangelo, Raphael, Titian, Rubens, Canova, Bernini and others. 480pp. 5⅜ x 8½. 27584-1

PSYCHOLOGY OF MUSIC, Carl E. Seashore. Classic work discusses music as a medium from psychological viewpoint. Clear treatment of physical acoustics, auditory apparatus, sound perception, development of musical skills, nature of musical feeling, host of other topics. 88 figures. 408pp. 5⅜ x 8½. 21851-1

THE PHILOSOPHY OF HISTORY, Georg W. Hegel. Great classic of Western thought develops concept that history is not chance but rational process, the evolution of freedom. 457pp. 5⅜ x 8½. 20112-0

THE BOOK OF TEA, Kakuzo Okakura. Minor classic of the Orient: entertaining, charming explanation, interpretation of traditional Japanese culture in terms of tea ceremony. 94pp. 5⅜ x 8½. 20070-1

LIFE IN ANCIENT EGYPT, Adolf Erman. Fullest, most thorough, detailed older account with much not in more recent books, domestic life, religion, magic, medicine, commerce, much more. Many illustrations reproduce tomb paintings, carvings, hieroglyphs, etc. 597pp. 5⅜ x 8½. 22632-8

SUNDIALS, Their Theory and Construction, Albert Waugh. Far and away the best, most thorough coverage of ideas, mathematics concerned, types, construction, adjusting anywhere. Simple, nontechnical treatment allows even children to build several of these dials. Over 100 illustrations. 230pp. 5⅜ x 8½. 22947-5

THEORETICAL HYDRODYNAMICS, L. M. Milne-Thomson. Classic exposition of the mathematical theory of fluid motion, applicable to both hydrodynamics and aerodynamics. Over 600 exercises. 768pp. 6⅛ x 9¼. 68970-0

SONGS OF EXPERIENCE: Facsimile Reproduction with 26 Plates in Full Color, William Blake. 26 full-color plates from a rare 1826 edition. Includes "The Tyger," "London," "Holy Thursday," and other poems. Printed text of poems. 48pp. 5¼ x 7. 24636-1

OLD-TIME VIGNETTES IN FULL COLOR, Carol Belanger Grafton (ed.). Over 390 charming, often sentimental illustrations, selected from archives of Victorian graphics—pretty women posing, children playing, food, flowers, kittens and puppies, smiling cherubs, birds and butterflies, much more. All copyright-free. 48pp. 9¼ x 12¼. 27269-9

PERSPECTIVE FOR ARTISTS, Rex Vicat Cole. Depth, perspective of sky and sea, shadows, much more, not usually covered. 391 diagrams, 81 reproductions of drawings and paintings. 279pp. 5⅜ x 8½. 22487-2

DRAWING THE LIVING FIGURE, Joseph Sheppard. Innovative approach to artistic anatomy focuses on specifics of surface anatomy, rather than muscles and bones. Over 170 drawings of live models in front, back and side views, and in widely varying poses. Accompanying diagrams. 177 illustrations. Introduction. Index. 144pp. 8⅜ x11¼. 26723-7

GOTHIC AND OLD ENGLISH ALPHABETS: 100 Complete Fonts, Dan X. Solo. Add power, elegance to posters, signs, other graphics with 100 stunning copyright-free alphabets: Blackstone, Dolbey, Germania, 97 more–including many lower-case, numerals, punctuation marks. 104pp. 8⅛ x 11. 24695-7

HOW TO DO BEADWORK, Mary White. Fundamental book on craft from simple projects to five-bead chains and woven works. 106 illustrations. 142pp. 5⅜ x 8. 20697-1

THE BOOK OF WOOD CARVING, Charles Marshall Sayers. Finest book for beginners discusses fundamentals and offers 34 designs. "Absolutely first rate . . . well thought out and well executed."–E. J. Tangerman. 118pp. 7¾ x 10⅝. 23654-4

ILLUSTRATED CATALOG OF CIVIL WAR MILITARY GOODS: Union Army Weapons, Insignia, Uniform Accessories, and Other Equipment, Schuyler, Hartley, and Graham. Rare, profusely illustrated 1846 catalog includes Union Army uniform and dress regulations, arms and ammunition, coats, insignia, flags, swords, rifles, etc. 226 illustrations. 160pp. 9 x 12. 24939-5

WOMEN'S FASHIONS OF THE EARLY 1900s: An Unabridged Republication of "New York Fashions, 1909," National Cloak & Suit Co. Rare catalog of mail-order fashions documents women's and children's clothing styles shortly after the turn of the century. Captions offer full descriptions, prices. Invaluable resource for fashion, costume historians. Approximately 725 illustrations. 128pp. 8⅜ x 11¼. 27276-1

THE 1912 AND 1915 GUSTAV STICKLEY FURNITURE CATALOGS, Gustav Stickley. With over 200 detailed illustrations and descriptions, these two catalogs are essential reading and reference materials and identification guides for Stickley furniture. Captions cite materials, dimensions and prices. 112pp. 6½ x 9¼. 26676-1

EARLY AMERICAN LOCOMOTIVES, John H. White, Jr. Finest locomotive engravings from early 19th century: historical (1804–74), main-line (after 1870), special, foreign, etc. 147 plates. 142pp. 11⅜ x 8¼. 22772-3

THE TALL SHIPS OF TODAY IN PHOTOGRAPHS, Frank O. Braynard. Lavishly illustrated tribute to nearly 100 majestic contemporary sailing vessels: Amerigo Vespucci, Clearwater, Constitution, Eagle, Mayflower, Sea Cloud, Victory, many more. Authoritative captions provide statistics, background on each ship. 190 black-and-white photographs and illustrations. Introduction. 128pp. 8⅞ x 11¾. 27163-3

LITTLE BOOK OF EARLY AMERICAN CRAFTS AND TRADES, Peter Stockham (ed.). 1807 children's book explains crafts and trades: baker, hatter, cooper, potter, and many others. 23 copperplate illustrations. 140pp. 4⅝ x 6.   23336-7

VICTORIAN FASHIONS AND COSTUMES FROM HARPER'S BAZAR, 1867–1898, Stella Blum (ed.). Day costumes, evening wear, sports clothes, shoes, hats, other accessories in over 1,000 detailed engravings. 320pp. 9⅜ x 12¼.   22990-4

GUSTAV STICKLEY, THE CRAFTSMAN, Mary Ann Smith. Superb study surveys broad scope of Stickley's achievement, especially in architecture. Design philosophy, rise and fall of the Craftsman empire, descriptions and floor plans for many Craftsman houses, more. 86 black-and-white halftones. 31 line illustrations. Introduction 208pp. 6½ x 9¼.   27210-9

THE LONG ISLAND RAIL ROAD IN EARLY PHOTOGRAPHS, Ron Ziel. Over 220 rare photos, informative text document origin (1844) and development of rail service on Long Island. Vintage views of early trains, locomotives, stations, passengers, crews, much more. Captions. 8⅞ x 11¾.   26301-0

VOYAGE OF THE LIBERDADE, Joshua Slocum. Great 19th-century mariner's thrilling, first-hand account of the wreck of his ship off South America, the 35-foot boat he built from the wreckage, and its remarkable voyage home. 128pp. 5⅜ x 8½.
40022-0

TEN BOOKS ON ARCHITECTURE, Vitruvius. The most important book ever written on architecture. Early Roman aesthetics, technology, classical orders, site selection, all other aspects. Morgan translation. 331pp. 5⅜ x 8½.   20645-9

THE HUMAN FIGURE IN MOTION, Eadweard Muybridge. More than 4,500 stopped-action photos, in action series, showing undraped men, women, children jumping, lying down, throwing, sitting, wrestling, carrying, etc. 390pp. 7⅞ x 10⅝.
20204-6 Clothbd.

TREES OF THE EASTERN AND CENTRAL UNITED STATES AND CANADA, William M. Harlow. Best one-volume guide to 140 trees. Full descriptions, woodlore, range, etc. Over 600 illustrations. Handy size. 288pp. 4½ x 6⅜.   20395-6

SONGS OF WESTERN BIRDS, Dr. Donald J. Borror. Complete song and call repertoire of 60 western species, including flycatchers, juncoes, cactus wrens, many more–includes fully illustrated booklet.   Cassette and manual 99913-0

GROWING AND USING HERBS AND SPICES, Milo Miloradovich. Versatile handbook provides all the information needed for cultivation and use of all the herbs and spices available in North America. 4 illustrations. Index. Glossary. 236pp. 5⅜ x 8½.
25058-X

BIG BOOK OF MAZES AND LABYRINTHS, Walter Shepherd. 50 mazes and labyrinths in all–classical, solid, ripple, and more–in one great volume. Perfect inexpensive puzzler for clever youngsters. Full solutions. 112pp. 8⅛ x 11.   22951-3

PIANO TUNING, J. Cree Fischer. Clearest, best book for beginner, amateur. Simple repairs, raising dropped notes, tuning by easy method of flattened fifths. No previous skills needed. 4 illustrations. 201pp. 5⅜ x 8½.   23267-0

HINTS TO SINGERS, Lillian Nordica. Selecting the right teacher, developing confidence, overcoming stage fright, and many other important skills receive thoughtful discussion in this indispensible guide, written by a world-famous diva of four decades' experience. 96pp. 5⅜ x 8½.   40094-8

THE COMPLETE NONSENSE OF EDWARD LEAR, Edward Lear. All nonsense limericks, zany alphabets, Owl and Pussycat, songs, nonsense botany, etc., illustrated by Lear. Total of 320pp. 5⅜ x 8½. (Available in U.S. only.)   20167-8

VICTORIAN PARLOUR POETRY: An Annotated Anthology, Michael R. Turner. 117 gems by Longfellow, Tennyson, Browning, many lesser-known poets. "The Village Blacksmith," "Curfew Must Not Ring Tonight," "Only a Baby Small," dozens more, often difficult to find elsewhere. Index of poets, titles, first lines. xxiii + 325pp. 5⅜ x 8¼.   27044-0

DUBLINERS, James Joyce. Fifteen stories offer vivid, tightly focused observations of the lives of Dublin's poorer classes. At least one, "The Dead," is considered a masterpiece. Reprinted complete and unabridged from standard edition. 160pp. 5³⁄₁₆ x 8¼.
26870-5

GREAT WEIRD TALES: 14 Stories by Lovecraft, Blackwood, Machen and Others, S. T. Joshi (ed.). 14 spellbinding tales, including "The Sin Eater," by Fiona McLeod, "The Eye Above the Mantel," by Frank Belknap Long, as well as renowned works by R. H. Barlow, Lord Dunsany, Arthur Machen, W. C. Morrow and eight other masters of the genre. 256pp. 5⅜ x 8½. (Available in U.S. only.)   40436-6

THE BOOK OF THE SACRED MAGIC OF ABRAMELIN THE MAGE, translated by S. MacGregor Mathers. Medieval manuscript of ceremonial magic. Basic document in Aleister Crowley, Golden Dawn groups. 268pp. 5⅜ x 8½.   23211-5

NEW RUSSIAN-ENGLISH AND ENGLISH-RUSSIAN DICTIONARY, M. A. O'Brien. This is a remarkably handy Russian dictionary, containing a surprising amount of information, including over 70,000 entries. 366pp. 4½ x 6¼.   20208-9

HISTORIC HOMES OF THE AMERICAN PRESIDENTS, Second, Revised Edition, Irvin Haas. A traveler's guide to American Presidential homes, most open to the public, depicting and describing homes occupied by every American President from George Washington to George Bush. With visiting hours, admission charges, travel routes. 175 photographs. Index. 160pp. 8¼ x 11.   26751-2

NEW YORK IN THE FORTIES, Andreas Feininger. 162 brilliant photographs by the well-known photographer, formerly with *Life* magazine. Commuters, shoppers, Times Square at night, much else from city at its peak. Captions by John von Hartz. 181pp. 9¼ x 10¾.   23585-8

INDIAN SIGN LANGUAGE, William Tomkins. Over 525 signs developed by Sioux and other tribes. Written instructions and diagrams. Also 290 pictographs. 111pp. 6⅛ x 9¼.   22029-X

ANATOMY: A Complete Guide for Artists, Joseph Sheppard. A master of figure drawing shows artists how to render human anatomy convincingly. Over 460 illustrations. 224pp. 8⅜ x 11¼. 27279-6

MEDIEVAL CALLIGRAPHY: Its History and Technique, Marc Drogin. Spirited history, comprehensive instruction manual covers 13 styles (ca. 4th century through 15th). Excellent photographs; directions for duplicating medieval techniques with modern tools. 224pp. 8⅜ x 11¼. 26142-5

DRIED FLOWERS: How to Prepare Them, Sarah Whitlock and Martha Rankin. Complete instructions on how to use silica gel, meal and borax, perlite aggregate, sand and borax, glycerine and water to create attractive permanent flower arrangements. 12 illustrations. 32pp. 5⅜ x 8½. 21802-3

EASY-TO-MAKE BIRD FEEDERS FOR WOODWORKERS, Scott D. Campbell. Detailed, simple-to-use guide for designing, constructing, caring for and using feeders. Text, illustrations for 12 classic and contemporary designs. 96pp. 5⅜ x 8½.
25847-5

SCOTTISH WONDER TALES FROM MYTH AND LEGEND, Donald A. Mackenzie. 16 lively tales tell of giants rumbling down mountainsides, of a magic wand that turns stone pillars into warriors, of gods and goddesses, evil hags, powerful forces and more. 240pp. 5⅜ x 8½. 29677-6

THE HISTORY OF UNDERCLOTHES, C. Willett Cunnington and Phyllis Cunnington. Fascinating, well-documented survey covering six centuries of English undergarments, enhanced with over 100 illustrations: 12th-century laced-up bodice, footed long drawers (1795), 19th-century bustles, 19th-century corsets for men, Victorian "bust improvers," much more. 272pp. 5⅜ x 8¼. 27124-2

ARTS AND CRAFTS FURNITURE: The Complete Brooks Catalog of 1912, Brooks Manufacturing Co. Photos and detailed descriptions of more than 150 now very collectible furniture designs from the Arts and Crafts movement depict davenports, settees, buffets, desks, tables, chairs, bedsteads, dressers and more, all built of solid, quarter-sawed oak. Invaluable for students and enthusiasts of antiques, Americana and the decorative arts. 80pp. 6½ x 9¼. 27471-3

WILBUR AND ORVILLE: A Biography of the Wright Brothers, Fred Howard. Definitive, crisply written study tells the full story of the brothers' lives and work. A vividly written biography, unparalleled in scope and color, that also captures the spirit of an extraordinary era. 560pp. 6⅛ x 9¼. 40297-5

THE ARTS OF THE SAILOR: Knotting, Splicing and Ropework, Hervey Garrett Smith. Indispensable shipboard reference covers tools, basic knots and useful hitches; handsewing and canvas work, more. Over 100 illustrations. Delightful reading for sea lovers. 256pp. 5⅜ x 8½. 26440-8

FRANK LLOYD WRIGHT'S FALLINGWATER: The House and Its History, Second, Revised Edition, Donald Hoffmann. A total revision–both in text and illustrations–of the standard document on Fallingwater, the boldest, most personal architectural statement of Wright's mature years, updated with valuable new material from the recently opened Frank Lloyd Wright Archives. "Fascinating"–*The New York Times*. 116 illustrations. 128pp. 9¼ x 10¾. 27430-6

PHOTOGRAPHIC SKETCHBOOK OF THE CIVIL WAR, Alexander Gardner. 100 photos taken on field during the Civil War. Famous shots of Manassas Harper's Ferry, Lincoln, Richmond, slave pens, etc. 244pp. 10⅝ x 8¼. 22731-6

FIVE ACRES AND INDEPENDENCE, Maurice G. Kains. Great back-to-the-land classic explains basics of self-sufficient farming. The one book to get. 95 illustrations. 397pp. 5⅜ x 8½. 20974-1

SONGS OF EASTERN BIRDS, Dr. Donald J. Borror. Songs and calls of 60 species most common to eastern U.S.: warblers, woodpeckers, flycatchers, thrushes, larks, many more in high-quality recording. Cassette and manual 99912-2

A MODERN HERBAL, Margaret Grieve. Much the fullest, most exact, most useful compilation of herbal material. Gigantic alphabetical encyclopedia, from aconite to zedoary, gives botanical information, medical properties, folklore, economic uses, much else. Indispensable to serious reader. 161 illustrations. 888pp. 6½ x 9¼. 2-vol. set. (Available in U.S. only.) Vol. I: 22798-7
Vol. II: 22799-5

HIDDEN TREASURE MAZE BOOK, Dave Phillips. Solve 34 challenging mazes accompanied by heroic tales of adventure. Evil dragons, people-eating plants, blood-thirsty giants, many more dangerous adversaries lurk at every twist and turn. 34 mazes, stories, solutions. 48pp. 8¼ x 11. 24566-7

LETTERS OF W. A. MOZART, Wolfgang A. Mozart. Remarkable letters show bawdy wit, humor, imagination, musical insights, contemporary musical world; includes some letters from Leopold Mozart. 276pp. 5⅜ x 8½. 22859-2

BASIC PRINCIPLES OF CLASSICAL BALLET, Agrippina Vaganova. Great Russian theoretician, teacher explains methods for teaching classical ballet. 118 illus-trations. 175pp. 5⅜ x 8½. 22036-2

THE JUMPING FROG, Mark Twain. Revenge edition. The original story of The Celebrated Jumping Frog of Calaveras County, a hapless French translation, and Twain's hilarious "retranslation" from the French. 12 illustrations. 66pp. 5⅜ x 8½. 22686-7

BEST REMEMBERED POEMS, Martin Gardner (ed.). The 126 poems in this superb collection of 19th- and 20th-century British and American verse range from Shelley's "To a Skylark" to the impassioned "Renascence" of Edna St. Vincent Millay and to Edward Lear's whimsical "The Owl and the Pussycat." 224pp. 5⅜ x 8½. 27165-X

COMPLETE SONNETS, William Shakespeare. Over 150 exquisite poems deal with love, friendship, the tyranny of time, beauty's evanescence, death and other themes in language of remarkable power, precision and beauty. Glossary of archaic terms. 80pp. 5³⁄₁₆ x 8¼. 26686-9

THE BATTLES THAT CHANGED HISTORY, Fletcher Pratt. Eminent historian profiles 16 crucial conflicts, ancient to modern, that changed the course of civiliza-tion. 352pp. 5⅜ x 8½. 41129-X

THE WIT AND HUMOR OF OSCAR WILDE, Alvin Redman (ed.). More than 1,000 ripostes, paradoxes, wisecracks: Work is the curse of the drinking classes; I can resist everything except temptation; etc. 258pp. 5⅜ x 8½.   20602-5

SHAKESPEARE LEXICON AND QUOTATION DICTIONARY, Alexander Schmidt. Full definitions, locations, shades of meaning in every word in plays and poems. More than 50,000 exact quotations. 1,485pp. 6½ x 9¼. 2-vol. set.

Vol. 1: 22726-X
Vol. 2: 22727-8

SELECTED POEMS, Emily Dickinson. Over 100 best-known, best-loved poems by one of America's foremost poets, reprinted from authoritative early editions. No comparable edition at this price. Index of first lines. 64pp. 5³⁄₁₆ x 8¼.   26466-1

THE INSIDIOUS DR. FU-MANCHU, Sax Rohmer. The first of the popular mystery series introduces a pair of English detectives to their archnemesis, the diabolical Dr. Fu-Manchu. Flavorful atmosphere, fast-paced action, and colorful characters enliven this classic of the genre. 208pp. 5³⁄₁₆ x 8¼.   29898-1

THE MALLEUS MALEFICARUM OF KRAMER AND SPRENGER, translated by Montague Summers. Full text of most important witchhunter's "bible," used by both Catholics and Protestants. 278pp. 6⅝ x 10.   22802-9

SPANISH STORIES/CUENTOS ESPAÑOLES: A Dual-Language Book, Angel Flores (ed.). Unique format offers 13 great stories in Spanish by Cervantes, Borges, others. Faithful English translations on facing pages. 352pp. 5⅜ x 8½.   25399-6

GARDEN CITY, LONG ISLAND, IN EARLY PHOTOGRAPHS, 1869–1919, Mildred H. Smith. Handsome treasury of 118 vintage pictures, accompanied by carefully researched captions, document the Garden City Hotel fire (1899), the Vanderbilt Cup Race (1908), the first airmail flight departing from the Nassau Boulevard Aerodrome (1911), and much more. 96pp. 8⅞ x 11¾.   40669-5

OLD QUEENS, N.Y., IN EARLY PHOTOGRAPHS, Vincent F. Seyfried and William Asadorian. Over 160 rare photographs of Maspeth, Jamaica, Jackson Heights, and other areas. Vintage views of DeWitt Clinton mansion, 1939 World's Fair and more. Captions. 192pp. 8⅞ x 11.   26358-4

CAPTURED BY THE INDIANS: 15 Firsthand Accounts, 1750-1870, Frederick Drimmer. Astounding true historical accounts of grisly torture, bloody conflicts, relentless pursuits, miraculous escapes and more, by people who lived to tell the tale. 384pp. 5⅜ x 8½.   24901-8

THE WORLD'S GREAT SPEECHES (Fourth Enlarged Edition), Lewis Copeland, Lawrence W. Lamm, and Stephen J. McKenna. Nearly 300 speeches provide public speakers with a wealth of updated quotes and inspiration—from Pericles' funeral oration and William Jennings Bryan's "Cross of Gold Speech" to Malcolm X's powerful words on the Black Revolution and Earl of Spenser's tribute to his sister, Diana, Princess of Wales. 944pp. 5⅜ x 8⅜.   40903-1

THE BOOK OF THE SWORD, Sir Richard F. Burton. Great Victorian scholar/adventurer's eloquent, erudite history of the "queen of weapons"—from prehistory to early Roman Empire. Evolution and development of early swords, variations (sabre, broadsword, cutlass, scimitar, etc.), much more. 336pp. 6⅛ x 9¼.

25434-8

AUTOBIOGRAPHY: The Story of My Experiments with Truth, Mohandas K. Gandhi. Boyhood, legal studies, purification, the growth of the Satyagraha (nonviolent protest) movement. Critical, inspiring work of the man responsible for the freedom of India. 480pp. 5⅜ x 8½. (Available in U.S. only.) 24593-4

CELTIC MYTHS AND LEGENDS, T. W. Rolleston. Masterful retelling of Irish and Welsh stories and tales. Cuchulain, King Arthur, Deirdre, the Grail, many more. First paperback edition. 58 full-page illustrations. 512pp. 5⅜ x 8½. 26507-2

THE PRINCIPLES OF PSYCHOLOGY, William James. Famous long course complete, unabridged. Stream of thought, time perception, memory, experimental methods; great work decades ahead of its time. 94 figures. 1,391pp. 5⅜ x 8½. 2-vol. set.
Vol. I: 20381-6   Vol. II: 20382-4

THE WORLD AS WILL AND REPRESENTATION, Arthur Schopenhauer. Definitive English translation of Schopenhauer's life work, correcting more than 1,000 errors, omissions in earlier translations. Translated by E. F. J. Payne. Total of 1,269pp. 5⅜ x 8½. 2-vol. set.
Vol. 1: 21761-2   Vol. 2: 21762-0

MAGIC AND MYSTERY IN TIBET, Madame Alexandra David-Neel. Experiences among lamas, magicians, sages, sorcerers, Bonpa wizards. A true psychic discovery. 32 illustrations. 321pp. 5⅜ x 8½. (Available in U.S. only.) 22682-4

THE EGYPTIAN BOOK OF THE DEAD, E. A. Wallis Budge. Complete reproduction of Ani's papyrus, finest ever found. Full hieroglyphic text, interlinear transliteration, word-for-word translation, smooth translation. 533pp. 6½ x 9¼. 21866-X

MATHEMATICS FOR THE NONMATHEMATICIAN, Morris Kline. Detailed, college-level treatment of mathematics in cultural and historical context, with numerous exercises. Recommended Reading Lists. Tables. Numerous figures. 641pp. 5⅜ x 8½. 24823-2

PROBABILISTIC METHODS IN THE THEORY OF STRUCTURES, Isaac Elishakoff. Well-written introduction covers the elements of the theory of probability from two or more random variables, the reliability of such multivariable structures, the theory of random function, Monte Carlo methods of treating problems incapable of exact solution, and more. Examples. 502pp. 5⅜ x 8½. 40691-1

THE RIME OF THE ANCIENT MARINER, Gustave Doré, S. T. Coleridge. Doré's finest work; 34 plates capture moods, subtleties of poem. Flawless full-size reproductions printed on facing pages with authoritative text of poem. "Beautiful. Simply beautiful."–Publisher's Weekly. 77pp. 9¼ x 12. 22305-1

NORTH AMERICAN INDIAN DESIGNS FOR ARTISTS AND CRAFTSPEOPLE, Eva Wilson. Over 360 authentic copyright-free designs adapted from Navajo blankets, Hopi pottery, Sioux buffalo hides, more. Geometrics, symbolic figures, plant and animal motifs, etc. 128pp. 8⅜ x 11. (Not for sale in the United Kingdom.) 25341-4

SCULPTURE: Principles and Practice, Louis Slobodkin. Step-by-step approach to clay, plaster, metals, stone; classical and modern. 253 drawings, photos. 255pp. 8⅛ x 11. 22960-2

THE INFLUENCE OF SEA POWER UPON HISTORY, 1660–1783, A. T. Mahan. Influential classic of naval history and tactics still used as text in war colleges. First paperback edition. 4 maps. 24 battle plans. 640pp. 5⅜ x 8½. 25509-3

THE STORY OF THE TITANIC AS TOLD BY ITS SURVIVORS, Jack Winocour (ed.). What it was really like. Panic, despair, shocking inefficiency, and a little heroism. More thrilling than any fictional account. 26 illustrations. 320pp. 5⅜ x 8½.
20610-6

FAIRY AND FOLK TALES OF THE IRISH PEASANTRY, William Butler Yeats (ed.). Treasury of 64 tales from the twilight world of Celtic myth and legend: "The Soul Cages," "The Kildare Pooka," "King O'Toole and his Goose," many more. Introduction and Notes by W. B. Yeats. 352pp. 5⅜ x 8½.
26941-8

BUDDHIST MAHAYANA TEXTS, E. B. Cowell and others (eds.). Superb, accurate translations of basic documents in Mahayana Buddhism, highly important in history of religions. The Buddha-karita of Asvaghosha, Larger Sukhavativyuha, more. 448pp. 5⅜ x 8½.
25552-2

ONE TWO THREE . . . INFINITY: Facts and Speculations of Science, George Gamow. Great physicist's fascinating, readable overview of contemporary science: number theory, relativity, fourth dimension, entropy, genes, atomic structure, much more. 128 illustrations. Index. 352pp. 5⅜ x 8½.
25664-2

EXPERIMENTATION AND MEASUREMENT, W. J. Youden. Introductory manual explains laws of measurement in simple terms and offers tips for achieving accuracy and minimizing errors. Mathematics of measurement, use of instruments, experimenting with machines. 1994 edition. Foreword. Preface. Introduction. Epilogue. Selected Readings. Glossary. Index. Tables and figures. 128pp. 5⅜ x 8½.
40451-X

DALÍ ON MODERN ART: The Cuckolds of Antiquated Modern Art, Salvador Dalí. Influential painter skewers modern art and its practitioners. Outrageous evaluations of Picasso, Cézanne, Turner, more. 15 renderings of paintings discussed. 44 calligraphic decorations by Dalí. 96pp. 5⅜ x 8½. (Available in U.S. only.)
29220-7

ANTIQUE PLAYING CARDS: A Pictorial History, Henry René D'Allemagne. Over 900 elaborate, decorative images from rare playing cards (14th–20th centuries): Bacchus, death, dancing dogs, hunting scenes, royal coats of arms, players cheating, much more. 96pp. 9¼ x 12¼.
29265-7

MAKING FURNITURE MASTERPIECES: 30 Projects with Measured Drawings, Franklin H. Gottshall. Step-by-step instructions, illustrations for constructing handsome, useful pieces, among them a Sheraton desk, Chippendale chair, Spanish desk, Queen Anne table and a William and Mary dressing mirror. 224pp. 8⅛ x 11¼.
29338-6

THE FOSSIL BOOK: A Record of Prehistoric Life, Patricia V. Rich et al. Profusely illustrated definitive guide covers everything from single-celled organisms and dinosaurs to birds and mammals and the interplay between climate and man. Over 1,500 illustrations. 760pp. 7½ x 10⅛.
29371-8